W9-BNF-634

Careers in Focus

Careers in Focus

CHEMISTRY

Ferguson
An imprint of Infobase Publishing

Careers in Focus: Chemistry

Copyright © 2008 by Infobase Publishing

Ferguson
An imprint of Infobase Publishing
132 West 31st Street
New York NY 10001

Library of Congress Cataloging-in-Publication Data

Careers in focus. Chemistry.
    p. cm.
    Includes bibliographical references and index.
    ISBN-13: 978-0-8160-7279-8 (hardcover: alk. paper)
    ISBN-10: 0-8160-7279-5 (hardcover: alk paper) 1. Chemistry—Vocational guidance—Juvenile literature. I. J.G. Ferguson Publishing Company.
    QD39.5.C245 2008
    540.23—dc22
                                    2007040867

Ferguson books are available at special discounts when purchased in bulk quantities for businesses, associations, institutions, or sales promotions. Please call our Special Sales Department in New York at (212) 967-8800 or (800) 322-8755.

You can find Ferguson on the World Wide Web at http://www.fergpubco.com

Text design by David Strelecky
Cover design by Salvatore Luongo

Printed in the United States of America

MP MSRF 10 9 8 7 6 5 4 3 2 1

This book is printed on acid-free paper.

Table of Contents

Introduction

Chemistry is the scientific study of the composition, changes, reactions, and transformations of matter. Many people who major in chemistry in college become chemists, chemical engineers and technicians, or college chemistry professors. Others combine their study of chemistry with classes or even dual majors in physics, environmental science, or biology, and pursue careers as environmental technicians, toxicologists, wood scientists, and a variety of other occupations.

The study of chemistry is an excellent path to well-paying, rewarding career opportunities that you might never have imagined. For example, you might work as a forensic expert gathering and analyzing evidence at a crime scene, a food technologist studying the chemical properties of tomatoes to improve their flavor and nutritional value, a pharmacologist developing a drug that will increase the life spans of people with pancreatic cancer, or a chemist at a petroleum company working to make the refining of petroleum less damaging to the environment.

In the United States, more than 881,000 people are employed in the chemical industry—a major employer of people with chemistry degrees. And nearly five million additional jobs are indirectly generated by the chemical industry, according to the American Chemical Society (ACS). Most of the 50,000-plus chemical products manufactured by the chemical and allied industries are used by other industries to make jet fuels, food additives, paints, detergents, and perfumes.

The chemical industry is a loose confederation of eight separate branches: agriculture, detergents, nitrogen compounds, paints, paper and textiles, petrochemicals, pharmaceuticals, and plastics. The occupational makeup of the workforce varies among the different branches of the chemical industry. Industries that make finished products ready for sale to the final consumer, such as paint and cosmetics, hire more administrative, marketing, and managerial personnel. A greater number of production workers are employed by industries that sell their products primarily to industrial consumers. The chemical industry is highly capital-intensive and has factories in practically every state. California, Illinois, New Jersey, New York, Ohio, Pennsylvania, South Carolina, Tennessee, and Texas have the most plants.

As a result of plant automation and more efficient production methods, job opportunities for production workers, who made up almost 44 percent of the total chemical industry workforce in 2004, are expected to decline. For those in the specialty occupations, including chemical engineers and chemical technicians, the employment outlook will be slightly better as the chemical manufacturing industry continues to research and develop new chemicals and streamline production processes for existing products. Employment for chemists will grow more slowly than the average for all occupations through 2014. Chemists who have at least a master's degree will be in the strongest demand. Opportunities for all workers will be best in pharmaceuticals and biotechnology and in research, development, and testing firms.

One area of strong growth is expected to be forensic chemistry, especially DNA analysis. According to the ACS, experts predict that more than 10,000 new forensic scientists will be needed over the next decade to work in private laboratories and government agencies. There is also a need for chemists to do crime-scene investigation and analysis of evidence.

Companies that provide environmental services and earth-friendly products should do well. This concern will also continue to compel the chemical industry to devote resources to complying with governmental regulations. Therefore, occupations related to compliance, improvement of product visibility, and promotion of consumer confidence should grow. International competitiveness will also be important.

Other trends include a continued emphasis on research and development. In order to stay competitive and differentiate their products, companies will continue to produce specialty chemicals, such as advanced polymers and plastics, which are designed for specific uses. This should increase employment of chemists in research-oriented positions. A focus on new manufacturing processes will also continue and should represent opportunities for chemical engineers. The market shift to specialty chemicals and increasing competition will create more marketing and sales positions as companies strive for product visibility and an increasing market niche. In general, opportunities in the chemical industry continue to be best for those with advanced degrees.

Each article in this book discusses in detail a particular chemistry-related occupation. The articles in *Careers in Focus: Chemistry* appear in Ferguson's *Encyclopedia of Careers and Vocational Guidance,* but have been updated and revised with the latest information from the U.S. Department of Labor, professional organizations, and other sources. The following paragraphs detail the sections and features that appear in the book.

The **Quick Facts** section provides a brief summary of the career including recommended school subjects, personal skills, work environment, minimum educational requirements, salary ranges, certification or licensing requirements, and employment outlook. This section also provides acronyms and identification numbers for the following government classification indexes: the *Dictionary of Occupational Titles* (DOT), the *Guide for Occupational Exploration* (GOE), the National Occupational Classification (NOC) Index, and the Occupational Information Network (O*NET)-Standard Occupational Classification System (SOC) index. The DOT, GOE, and O*NET-SOC indexes have been created by the U.S. government; the NOC index is Canada's career classification system. Readers can use the identification numbers listed in the Quick Facts section to access further information about a career. Print editions of the DOT (*Dictionary of Occupational Titles*. Indianapolis, Ind.: JIST Works, 1991) and GOE (*Guide for Occupational Exploration*. Indianapolis, Ind.: JIST Works, 2001) are available at libraries. Electronic versions of the NOC (http://www23.hrdc-drhc.gc.ca) and O*NET-SOC (http://online.onetcenter.org) are available on the Internet. When no DOT, GOE, NOC, or O*NET-SOC numbers are present, this means that the U.S. Department of Labor or Human Resources Development Canada have not created a numerical designation for this career. In this instance, you will see the acronym "N/A," or not available.

The **Overview** section is a brief introductory description of the duties and responsibilities involved in this career. Oftentimes, a career may have a variety of job titles. When this is the case, alternative career titles are presented. Employment statistics are also provided, when available. The **History** section describes the history of the particular job as it relates to the overall development of its industry or field. **The Job** describes the primary and secondary duties of the job. **Requirements** discusses high school and postsecondary education and training requirements, any certification or licensing that is necessary, and other personal requirements for success in the job. **Exploring** offers suggestions on how to gain experience in or knowledge of the particular job before making a firm educational and financial commitment. The focus is on what can be done while still in high school (or in the early years of college) to gain a better understanding of the job. The **Employers** section gives an overview of typical places of employment for the job. **Starting Out** discusses the best ways to land that first job, be it through the college career services office, newspaper ads, Internet employment sites, or personal contact. The **Advancement** section describes what kind of career path to expect from the job and how to get there. **Earnings** lists salary ranges and describes the typical fringe benefits. The **Work Environment** section describes the typical surroundings and conditions of employment—whether indoors or outdoors, noisy or quiet, social or independent. Also discussed are typical hours worked, any seasonal fluctuations, and the stresses and strains of the job. The **Outlook** section summarizes the job in terms of the general economy and industry projections. For the most part, Outlook information is obtained from the U.S. Bureau of Labor Statistics and is supplemented by information gathered from professional associations. Job growth terms follow those used in the *Occupational Outlook Handbook*. Growth described as "much faster than the average" means an increase of 27 percent or more. Growth described as "faster than the average" means an increase of 18 to 26 percent. Growth described as "about as fast as the average" means an increase of 9 to 17 percent. Growth described as "more slowly than the average" means an increase of 0 to 8 percent. "Decline" means a decrease by any amount. Each article ends with **For More Information,** which lists organizations that provide information on training, education, internships, scholarships, and job placement.

Careers in Focus: Chemistry also includes photographs, informative sidebars, and interviews with professionals in the field.

Agricultural Scientists

OVERVIEW

Agricultural scientists study all aspects of living organisms and the relationships of plants and animals to their environment. They conduct basic research in laboratories or in the field. They apply the results to such tasks as increasing crop yields and improving the environment. Some agricultural scientists plan and administer programs for testing foods, drugs, and other products. Others direct activities at public exhibits at such places as zoos and botanical gardens. Some agricultural scientists are professors at colleges and universities or work as consultants to business firms or the government. Others work in technical sales and service jobs for manufacturers of agricultural products. There are approximately 30,000 agricultural and food scientists in the United States; about 25 percent work for the federal, state, or local governments. Several thousand more are employed as university professors.

HISTORY

In 1840, Justius von Liebig of Germany published *Organic Chemistry in Its Applications to Agriculture and Physiology* and launched the systematic development of the agricultural sciences. A formal system of agricultural education soon followed in both Europe and the United States. Prior to the publication of this work, agricultural developments relied on the collective experience of farmers handed down over generations. Agricultural science has techniques in common with many other disciplines including biology, botany, genetics, nutrition, breeding, and engineering. Discoveries and improvements

QUICK FACTS

School Subjects
Biology
Chemistry

Personal Skills
Communication/ideas
Technical/scientific

Work Environment
Indoors and outdoors
Primarily multiple locations

Minimum Education Level
Bachelor's degree

Salary Range
$33,650 to $56,080 to
$93,460+

Certification or Licensing
Voluntary (certification)
Required for certain
positions (licensing)

Outlook
About as fast as the average

DOT
040

GOE
02.03.01, 02.03.02,
02.07.01

NOC
2121

O*NET-SOC
19-1011.00, 19-1013.01

in these fields contributed to advances in agriculture. Some milestones include the discovery of the practice of crop rotation and the application of manure as fertilizer, which greatly increased farm yields in the 1700s. Farm mechanization was greatly advanced by the invention of the mechanical reaper in 1831 and the gasoline tractor in 1892. Chemical fertilizers were first used in the 19th century; pesticides and herbicides soon followed. In 1900, the research of an Austrian monk, Gregor Johann Mendel, was rediscovered. His theories of plant characteristics, based on studies using generations of garden peas, formed the foundation for the science of genetics.

In the 20th century, scientists and engineers were at the forefront of farm, crop, and food processing improvements. Conservationist Gifford Pinchot developed some of the first methods to prevent soil erosion in 1910, and Clarence Birdseye perfected a method of freezing food in the 1920s. Birdseye's discoveries allowed for new crops of produce previously too perishable for the marketplace. By the 1960s, better quality feed and pesticides were in common use. Today, advances in genetic engineering and biotechnology are leading to more efficient, economical methods of farming and new markets for crops.

In recent years, agricultural scientists have played an important role in the development of ethanol, a clean-burning fuel that is created from renewable resources such as corn. Some scientists are encouraging the use of ethanol as a means to reduce U.S. dependence on oil from foreign countries and create more environmentally friendly energy options.

THE JOB

The nature of the work of the agricultural scientist can be broken down into several areas of specialization. Within each specialization are various careers.

The following are careers that fall under the areas of plant and soil science.

Agronomists investigate large-scale food-crop problems, conduct experiments, and develop new methods of growing crops to ensure more efficient production, higher yields, and improved quality. They use genetic engineering to develop crops that are resistant to pests, drought, and plant diseases.

Agronomists also engage in soil science. They analyze soils to find ways to increase production and reduce soil erosion. They study the responses of various soil types to fertilizers, tillage practices, and crop rotation. Since soil science is related to environmental science, agronomists may also use their expertise to consult with farmers and agricultural companies on environmental quality and effective land use.

Botanists are concerned with plants and their environment, structure, heredity, and economic value in such fields as agronomy, horticulture, and medicine.

Horticulturists study fruit and nut orchards as well as garden plants such as vegetables and flowers. They conduct experiments to develop new and improved varieties and to increase crop quality and yields. They also work to improve plant culture methods for the landscaping and beautification of communities, parks, and homes.

Plant breeders apply genetics and biotechnology to improve plants' yield, quality, and resistance to harsh weather, disease, and insects. They might work on developing strains of wild or cultivated plants that will have a larger yield and increase profits.

Plant pathologists research plant diseases and the decay of plant products to identify symptoms, determine causes, and develop control measures. They attempt to predict outbreaks by studying how different soils, climates, and geography affect the spread and intensity of plant disease.

Another area of specialization for agricultural scientists is animal science.

Animal scientists conduct research and develop improved methods for housing, breeding, feeding, and controlling diseases of domestic farm animals. They inspect and grade livestock food products, purchase livestock, or work in sales and marketing of livestock products. They often consult agricultural businesses on such areas as upgrading animal housing, lowering mortality rates, or increasing production of animal products such as milk and eggs.

Dairy scientists study the selection, breeding, feeding, and management of dairy cattle. For example, they research how various types of food and environmental conditions affect milk production and quality. They also develop new breeding programs to improve dairy herds.

Poultry scientists study the breeding, feeding, and management of poultry to improve the quantity and quality of eggs and other poultry products.

Animal breeders specialize in improving the quality of farm animals. They may work for a state agricultural department, agricultural extension station, or university. Some of their work is done in a laboratory, but much of it is done outdoors working directly on animals. Using their knowledge of genetics, animal breeders develop systems for animals to achieve desired characteristics such as strength, fast maturation, resistance to disease, and quality of meat.

Food science is a specialty closely related to animal science, but it focuses on meeting consumer demand for food products in ways that are healthy, safe, and convenient.

Food scientists use their backgrounds in chemistry, microbiology, and other sciences to develop new or better ways of preserving, packaging, processing, storing, and delivering foods. *Food technologists* work in product development to discover new food sources and analyze food content to determine levels of vitamins, fat, sugar, and protein. Food technologists also work to enforce government regulations, inspecting food processing areas and ensuring that sanitation, safety, quality, and waste management standards are met.

Much of the research conducted by agricultural scientists is done in laboratories and requires a familiarity with research techniques and the use of laboratory equipment and computers. Some research, however, is carried out wherever necessary. A botanist may have occasion to examine the plants that grow in the volcanic valleys of Alaska, or an animal breeder may study the behavior of animals on the plains of Africa.

REQUIREMENTS

High School

Follow your high school's college preparatory program, which will include courses in English, foreign language, mathematics, and government. Also take biology, chemistry, physics, and any other science courses available. You must also become familiar with basic computer skills, including programming. It may be possible for you to perform laboratory assistant duties for your science teachers. Visiting research laboratories and attending lectures by agricultural scientists can also be helpful.

Postsecondary Training

Educational requirements for agricultural scientists are very high. A doctorate is usually mandatory for careers as college or university professors, independent researchers, or field managers. A bachelor's degree may be acceptable for some entry-level jobs, such as testing or inspecting technicians, or as technical sales or service representatives. Promotions, however, are very limited for these employees unless they earn advanced degrees.

To become an agricultural scientist, you should pursue a degree related to agricultural and biological science. As an undergraduate, you should have a firm foundation in biology, with courses in chemistry, physics, mathematics, and English. Most colleges and universities have agricultural science curriculums, although liberal arts colleges may emphasize the biological sciences. State universities usually offer agricultural science programs, too.

While pursuing an advanced degree, you'll participate in research projects and write a dissertation on your specialized area of study. You'll also do fieldwork and laboratory research along with your classroom studies.

Certification or Licensing
The American Society of Agronomy offers several certifications, including the certified professional agronomist designation, to candidates based on their training and work. Contact the society for more information.

Other Requirements
As a researcher, you should be self-motivated enough to work effectively alone, yet be able to function cooperatively as part of a team. You should have an inexhaustible curiosity about the nature of living things and their environments. You must be systematic in your work habits and in your approach to investigation and experimentation and must have the persistence to continue or start over when experiments are not immediately successful.

Work performed by agricultural scientists in offices and laboratories requires intense powers of concentration and the ability to communicate one's thoughts systematically. In addition to these skills, physical stamina is necessary for those scientists who do field research in remote areas of the world.

EXPLORING

If you live in an agricultural community, you may be able to find part-time or summer work on a farm or ranch. Joining a chapter of the National FFA Organization (formerly Future Farmers of America) or a 4-H program will introduce you to the concerns of farmers and researchers and may involve you directly in science projects. Contact your county's extension office to learn about regional projects. You may also find part-time work in veterinarian's offices, florist shops, landscape nurseries, orchards, farms, zoos, aquariums, botanical gardens, or museums. Volunteer work is often available in zoos and animal shelters.

EMPLOYERS

About 25 percent of all agricultural and food scientists work for federal, state, and local governments. They work within the U.S. Department of Agriculture and the Environmental Protection Agency and for regional extension agencies and soil conservation departments. Scientists with doctorates may work on the faculty of colleges and universities. Researchers work for chemical and pharmaceutical companies, and with agribusiness and consulting firms. Agricultural scientists also work in the food processing industry.

STARTING OUT

Agricultural scientists often are recruited prior to graduation. College and university career services offices offer information about jobs, and students may arrange interviews with recruiters who visit the campus.

Direct application may be made to the personnel departments of colleges and universities, private industries, and nonprofit research foundations. People interested in positions with the federal government may contact the local offices of state employment services and the U.S. Office of Personnel Management (http://www.usajobs.opm. gov), which are located in various large cities throughout the country. Private employment agencies are another method that might be considered. Large companies sometimes conduct job fairs in major cities and will advertise them in the business sections of the local newspapers.

ADVANCEMENT

Advancement in this field depends on education, experience, and job performance. Agricultural scientists with advanced degrees generally start in teaching or research and advance to administrative and management positions, such as supervisor of a research program. The number of such jobs is limited, however, and often the route to advancement is through specialization. The narrower specialties are often the most valuable.

People who enter this field with only a bachelor's degree are much more restricted. After starting in testing and inspecting jobs or as technical sales and service representatives, they may progress to advanced technicians, particularly in medical research, or become high school biology teachers. In the latter case, they must have had courses in education and meet the state requirements for teaching credentials.

EARNINGS

According to the U.S. Department of Labor, the median annual salary of soil and plant scientists was approximately $56,080 in 2006. The lowest paid 10 percent (which generally included those just starting out in the field) earned less than $33,650, while the highest paid 10 percent made approximately $93,460 or more per year.

Unless hired for just a short-term project, agricultural scientists most likely receive health and retirement benefits in addition to their annual salary.

WORK ENVIRONMENT

Agricultural scientists work regular hours, although researchers often choose to work longer when their experiments have reached critical points. Competition in the research field may be stiff, causing a certain amount of stress.

Agricultural scientists generally work in offices, laboratories, or classrooms where the environment is clean, healthy, and safe. Some agricultural scientists, such as botanists, periodically take field trips where living conditions may be primitive and strenuous physical activity may be required.

OUTLOOK

According to the U.S. Department of Labor, employment for agricultural scientists is expected to grow about as fast as the average for all occupations through 2014. The fields of biotechnology, genetics, and sustainable agriculture may hold the best opportunities for agricultural scientists. New developments, such as methods of processing corn for use in medicines and for fuel for motor vehicles, will alter the marketplace. Scientists will also be actively involved in improving both the environmental impact of farming and crop yields, as they focus on methods of decontaminating soil, protecting groundwater, crop rotation, and other efforts of conservation. Scientists will also have the challenge of promoting these new methods to farmers.

FOR MORE INFORMATION

To learn about opportunities for scientists in the dairy industry and for information on student divisions at the college level, contact
American Dairy Science Association
1111 North Dunlap Avenue
Savoy, IL 61874-9604
Tel: 217-356-5146
Email: adsa@assochq.org
http://www.adsa.org

For information on careers and certification, contact
American Society of Agronomy
677 South Segoe Road
Madison, WI 53711-1086
Tel: 608-273-8080
http://www.agronomy.org

For more information on agricultural careers and student programs, contact
National FFA Organization
6060 FFA Drive
PO Box 68960
Indianapolis, IN 46268-0960
Tel: 317-802-6060
http://www.ffa.org

Visit the USDA Web site for more information on its agencies and programs as well as news releases.
United States Department of Agriculture (USDA)
http://www.usda.gov

Biochemists

OVERVIEW

Biochemists explore the tiny world of the cell, study how illnesses develop, and search for ways to improve life on earth. Through studying the chemical makeup of living organisms, biochemists strive to understand the dynamics of life, from the secrets of cell-to-cell communication to the chemical changes in our brains that give us memories. Biochemists examine the chemical combinations and reactions involved in such functions as growth, metabolism, reproduction, and heredity. They also study the effect of environment on living tissue. If cancer is to be cured, the earth's pollution cleaned up, or the aging process slowed, it will be biochemists and molecular biologists who will lead the way.

HISTORY

Biochemistry is a fairly new science, even though the concept of biochemistry is said to have its roots in the discovery of the fermentation process thousands of years ago. In fact, the basic steps used to make wine from grapes were the same in ancient times as they are today. However, the rather unchanging methods used for alcohol fermentation do not nearly reflect the revolutionary changes that have occurred throughout recent history in our knowledge of cell composition, growth, and function.

Robert Hooke, an English scientist, first described and named cells in 1665, when he looked at a slice of bark from an oak tree under a microscope with a magnifying power of 30x. Hooke never realized the significance of his discovery, however, because he thought the tiny boxes or "cells" he saw were unique to the bark. Anton van Leeuwenhoek, a Dutchman who lived in Hooke's time,

QUICK FACTS

School Subjects
Biology
Chemistry

Personal Skills
Mechanical/manipulative
Technical/scientific

Work Environment
Primarily indoors
Primarily one location

Minimum Education Level
Bachelor's degree

Salary Range
$31,258 to $76,320 to $129,510+

Certification or Licensing
Required for certain positions

Outlook
About as fast as the average

DOT
041

GOE
02.03.03

NOC
2112

O*NET-SOC
19-1021.00, 19-1021.01

discovered the existence of single-celled organisms by observing them in pond water and in animal blood and sperm. He used grains of sand that he had polished into magnifying glasses as powerful as 300x to see this invisible world. In 1839, nearly two centuries after Hooke's and Leeuwenhoek's discoveries, two German biologists, Matthias Schleiden and Theodor Schwann, correctly concluded that all living things consisted of cells. This theory was later expanded to include the idea that all cells come from other cells, and that the ability of cells to divide to form new cells is the basis for all reproduction, growth, and repair of many-celled organisms, like humans.

Over the past decades, a powerful instrument called the electron microscope has revealed the complex structure of cells. Every cell, at some state in its life, contains deoxyribonucleic acid, or DNA, the genetic material that directs the cell's many activities. Biochemists have widened their scope to include the study of protein molecules and chromosomes, the building blocks of life itself. Biology and chemistry have always been allied sciences, and the exploration of cells and their molecular components, carried out by biochemists and other biological scientists, has revealed much about life. Watson and Crick's breakthrough discovery of the structure of DNA in 1953 touched off a flurry of scientific activity that led to a better and better understanding of DNA chemistry and the genetic code. These discoveries eventually made it possible to manipulate DNA, enabling genetic engineers to transplant foreign genes into microorganisms to produce such valuable products as human insulin, which occurred in 1982.

Today, the field of biochemistry crosses over into many other sciences, as biochemists have become involved in genetics, nutrition, psychology, fertility, agriculture, and more. The new biotechnology is revolutionizing the pharmaceutical industry. Much of this work is done by biochemists and molecular biologists because this technology involves understanding the complex chemistry of life.

THE JOB

Depending on their education level and area of specialty, biochemists can do many types of work for a variety of employers. For instance, a biochemist could do basic research for a federal government agency or for individual states with laboratories that employ skilled persons to analyze food, drug, air, water, waste, or animal tissue samples. A biochemist might work for a drug company as part of a basic research team searching for the cause of diseases or conduct applied research to develop drugs to cure disease. A biochemist might work in a biotechnology company focusing on the environment, energy, human health care, agriculture, or animal health. There, he or she might do research or quality control, or work on manufacturing/production or information systems. Another possibility is for the biochemist to specialize in an additional area, such as law, business, or journalism, and use his or her biochemistry or molecular biology background for a career that combines science with regulatory affairs, management, writing, or teaching.

Ph.D. scientists who enter the highest levels of academic life combine teaching and research. In addition to teaching in university classrooms and laboratories, they also do basic research designed to increase biochemistry and molecular biology knowledge. As Ph.D. scientists, these professionals could also work for an industry or government laboratory doing basic research or research and development (R&D). The problems studied, research styles, and type of organization vary widely across different laboratories. The Ph.D. scientist may lead a research group or be part of a small team of Ph.D. researchers. Other Ph.D. scientists might opt for administrative positions. In government, for example, these scientists might lead programs concerned with the safety of new devices, food, drugs, or pesticides and other chemicals. Or they might influence which projects will get federal funding.

Generally, biochemists employed in the United States work in one of three major fields: medicine, nutrition, or agriculture. In medicine, biochemists mass-produce life-saving chemicals usually found only in minuscule amounts in the body. Some of these chemicals have helped diabetics and heart attack victims for years. Biochemists employed in the field of medicine might work to identify chemical changes in organs or cells that signal the development of such diseases as cancer, diabetes, or schizophrenia. Or they may look for chemical explanations for why certain people develop muscular dystrophy or become obese. While studying chemical makeup and changes in these situations, biochemists may work to discover a treatment or a prevention for a disease. For instance, biochemists discovering how certain diseases such as AIDS and cancer escape detection by the immune system are also devising ways to enhance immunity to fight these diseases. Biochemists are also finding out the chemical basis of fertility and how to improve the success of in vitro fertilization to help couples have children or to preserve endangered species.

Biochemists in the pharmaceutical industry design, develop, and evaluate drugs, antibiotics, diagnostic kits, and other medical devices. They may search out ways to produce antibiotics, hormones, enzymes, or other drug components, or they may do quality control on the way in which drugs and dosages are made and determined.

In the field of nutrition, biochemists examine the effects of food on the body. For example, they might study the relationship between diet and diabetes. Biochemists doing this study could look at the nutrition content of certain foods eaten by people with diabetes and study how these foods affect the functioning of the pancreas and other organs. Biochemists in the nutrition field also look at vitamin and mineral deficiencies and how they affect the human body. They examine these deficiencies in relation to body performance, and they may study anything from how the liver is affected by a lack of vitamin B to the effects of poor nutrition on the ability to learn.

Biochemists involved in agriculture undertake studies to discover more efficient methods of crop cultivation, storage, and pest control. For example, they might create genetically engineered crops that are more resistant to frost, drought, spoilage, disease, and pests. They might focus on helping to create fruit trees that produce more fruit by studying the biochemical composition of the plant and determining how to alter or select for this desirable trait. Biochemists may study the chemical composition of insects to determine better and more efficient methods of controlling the pest population and the damage they do to crops. Or they could work on programming bacteria to clean up the environment by "eating" toxic chemicals.

About seven out of 10 biochemists are engaged in basic research, often for a university medical school or nonprofit organization, such as a foundation or research institute. The remaining 30 percent do applied research, using the discoveries of basic research to solve practical problems or develop products. For example, a biochemist working in basic research may make a discovery about how a living organism forms hormones. This discovery will lead to a scientist doing applied research, making hormones in the laboratory, and eventually to mass production. Discoveries made in DNA research have led to techniques for identifying criminals from a single strand of hair or a tiny blood stain left at the scene of a crime. The distinction between basic and applied research is one of degree, however; biochemists often engage in both types of work.

Biochemistry requires skillful use of a wide range of sophisticated analytical equipment and application of newly discovered techniques requiring special instruments or new chemical reagents. Sometimes, biochemists themselves must invent and test new instruments if existing methods and equipment do not meet their needs.

Books to Read: Chemistry Experiments

Ebbing, Darrell D. *Experiments In General Chemistry.* 8th ed. Boston: Houghton Mifflin Company, 2006.

Garland, Carl W., Joseph W. Nibler, and David P. Shoemaker. *Experiments in Physical Chemistry.* 7th ed. New York: McGraw-Hill Science/Engineering/Math, 2006.

Herr, Norman, and James Cunningham. *Hands-On Chemistry Activities with Real-Life Applications: Easy-to-Use Labs and Demonstrations for Grades 8-12.* San Francisco: Jossey-Bass, 1999.

Murov, Steven, and Brian Stedjee. *Experiments and Exercises in Basic Chemistry.* 6th ed. Hoboken, N.J.: Wiley, 2003.

Rohrig, Brian. *150 Captivating Chemistry Experiments Using Household Substances.* Rev. ed. Plain City, Ohio: FizzBang Science, 2002.

———. *150 More Captivating Chemistry Experiments Using Household Substances.* Plain City, Ohio: FizzBang Science, 2002.

Biochemists must also be patient, methodical, and careful in their laboratory procedures.

REQUIREMENTS

Although they usually specialize in one of many areas in the field, biochemists and molecular biologists should also be familiar with several scientific disciplines, including chemistry, physics, mathematics, and computer science. High school classes can provide the foundation for getting this knowledge, while four years of college expands it, and postgraduate work directs students to explore specific areas more deeply. The following describes possible strategies at each level and includes a community college option.

High School

If you have an interest in biochemistry as a high school student, you should take at least one year each of biology, chemistry, physics, algebra, geometry, and trigonometry. Introductory calculus is also a good idea. Because scientists must clearly and accurately communicate their results verbally and in writing, English courses that emphasize writing skills are strongly recommended. Many colleges and universities also require several years of a foreign language, a useful skill today, as scientists frequently exchange information with researchers from other countries.

Postsecondary Training

Some colleges have their own special requirements for admission, so you should do a little research and take any special courses you need for the college that interests you. Also, check the catalogs of colleges and universities to see if they offer a program in biochemistry or related sciences. Some schools award a bachelor's degree in biochemistry, and nearly all colleges and universities offer a major in biology or chemistry.

To best prepare yourself for a career in biochemistry or molecular biology, you should start by earning a bachelor's degree in either of these two areas. Even if your college does not offer a specific program in biochemistry or molecular biology, you can get comparable training by doing one of two things: (1) working toward a bachelor's degree in chemistry and taking courses in biology, molecular genetics, and biochemistry, including a biochemistry laboratory class, or (2) earning a bachelor's degree in biology, but taking more chemistry, mathematics, and physics courses than the biology major may require, and also choosing a biochemistry course that has lab work with it.

It really doesn't matter if you earn a bachelor of science (B.S.) or a bachelor of arts (B.A.) degree; some schools offer both. It is more important to choose your courses thoughtfully and to get advice in your freshman year from a faculty member who knows about the fields of biochemistry and molecular biology.

Many careers in biochemistry, especially those that involve teaching at a college or directing scientific research at a university, a government laboratory, or a commercial company, require at least a master's degree and prefer a doctorate or Ph.D. degree. Most students enter graduate programs with a bachelor's degree in biochemistry, or in chemistry or biology with supplementary courses. Because biochemistry and molecular biology are so broad-based, you can enter their graduate programs from such diverse fields as physics, psychology, nutrition, microbiology, or engineering. Graduate schools prefer students with laboratory or research experience.

However you get there, a graduate education program is intense. A master's degree requires about a year of course work and often a research project as well. For a Ph.D. degree, full-time course work can last up to two years, followed by one or more special test exams. But the most important part of Ph.D. training is the requirement for all students to conduct an extensive research project leading to significant new scientific findings. Most students work under a faculty member's direction. This training is vital, as it will help you develop the skills to frame scientific questions and discover ways to

Chemistry students in a lab perform an experiment that determines the weight of a product of a chemical reaction. *(David Lassman, Syracuse Newspapers, The Image Works)*

answer them. It will also teach you important laboratory skills useful in tackling other biochemical problems. Most students complete a Ph.D. program in four or five years.

Certification or Licensing
Biochemists who wish to work in a hospital may need certification by a national certifying board such as the American Board of Clinical Chemistry.

Other Requirements
A scientist never stops learning, even when formal education has ended. This is particularly true for biochemists and molecular biologists because constant breakthroughs and technology advances make for a constantly changing work environment. That is why most Ph.D.'s go for more research experience (postdoctoral research) before they enter the workplace. As a "postdoc," you would not take course work, earn a degree, or teach; you would likely work full time on a high-level research project in the laboratory of an established scientist. Typically, this postdoctoral period lasts two to three years, during which time you would get a salary or be supported by a fellowship. Though not essential for many industry research jobs, postdoctoral research is generally expected of those wishing

to become professors. Also, because biochemistry and medicine are such allies, some Ph.D. recipients also earn their medical degrees, or M.D.'s, as a physician does. This is to get the broadest possible base for a career in medical research.

EXPLORING

The analytical, specialized nature of most biochemistry makes it unlikely that you will gain much exposure to it before college. Many high school chemistry and biology courses, however, allow students to work with laboratory tools and techniques that will give them a valuable background before college. In some cases, high school students can take advantage of opportunities to train as laboratory technicians by taking courses at a community college. You might also want to contact local colleges, universities, or laboratories to set up interviews with biochemists to learn as much as you can about the field. In addition, reading science and medical magazines will help you to stay current with recent breakthroughs in the biochemistry field.

EMPLOYERS

Government agencies at the federal, state, and local levels employ more than 50 percent of all biological scientists. At such agencies these scientists may do basic research and analyze food, drug, air, water, waste, or animal tissue samples. Biochemists also work for university medical schools or nonprofit organizations, such as a foundation or research institute, doing basic research. Drug companies employ biochemists to search for the causes of diseases or develop drugs to cure them. Biochemists work in quality control, research, manufacturing/production, or information systems at biotechnology companies that concentrate on the environment, energy, human health care, agriculture, or animal health. Universities hire biochemists to teach in combination with doing research.

STARTING OUT

A bachelor's degree in biochemistry or molecular biology can help you get into medical, dental, veterinary, law, or business school. It can also be a stepping-stone to a career in many different but related fields: biotechnology, toxicology, biomedical engineering, clinical chemistry, plant pathology, animal science, or other fields. Biochemists fresh from a college undergraduate program can take advantage of opportunities to get valuable on-the-job experience in a biochemistry or molecular biology laboratory. The National Science Foundation and the National Institutes of Health, both federal government agencies, sponsor research programs for undergraduates. Groups who can particularly benefit from these programs include women, Hispanic Americans, African Americans, Native Americans, Native Alaskans, and students with disabilities. Your college or university may also offer senior research projects that provide hands-on experience.

Another way to improve your chances of getting a job is to spend an additional year at a university with training programs for specialized laboratory techniques. Researchers and companies like these "certificate programs" because they teach valuable skills related to cell culture, genetic engineering, recombinant DNA technology, biotechnology, in vitro cell biology, protein engineering, or DNA sequencing and synthesis. In some universities, you can work toward a bachelor's degree and a certificate at the same time.

Biochemists with a bachelor's degree usually begin work in industry or government as research assistants doing testing and analysis. In the drug industry, for example, you might analyze the ingredients of a product to verify and maintain its quality. Biochemists with a master's degree may enter the field in management, marketing, or sales positions, whereas those with a doctorate usually go into basic or applied research. Many Ph.D. graduates work at colleges and universities where the emphasis is on teaching.

ADVANCEMENT

The more education you have, the greater your reward potential. Biochemists with a graduate degree have more opportunities for advancement than those with only an undergraduate degree. It is not uncommon for students to go back to graduate school after working for a while in a job that required a lesser degree. Some graduate students become research or teaching assistants in colleges and universities, qualifying for professorships when they receive their advanced degrees. Having a doctorate allows you to design research initiatives and direct others in carrying out experiments. Experienced biochemists with doctorates can move up to high-level administrative positions and supervise entire research programs. Other highly qualified biochemists who prefer to devote themselves to research often become leaders in a particular aspect of their profession.

EARNINGS

According to a report by the National Association of Colleges and Employers, beginning salaries in 2005 for graduates with bachelor's degrees in biological science averaged $31,258 per year.

The U.S. Department of Labor reports that biochemists and biophysicists earned average annual incomes of $76,320 in 2006. Salaries ranged from less than $40,820 to more than $129,510 per year.

Colleges and universities also employ many biochemists as professors and researchers. The U.S. Department of Labor reports that postsecondary chemistry teachers earned salaries that ranged from less than $36,160 to more than $116,910 in 2006. College biology teachers had earnings that ranged from less than $37,620 to more than $101,780.

Biochemists who work for universities, the government, or industry all tend to receive good benefits packages, such as health and life insurance, pension plans, and paid vacation and sick leave. Those employed as university faculty operate on the academic calendar, which means that they can get summer and winter breaks from teaching classes.

WORK ENVIRONMENT

Biochemists generally work in clean, quiet, and well-lighted laboratories where physical labor is minimal. They must, however, take the proper precautions in handling chemicals and organic substances that could be dangerous or cause illness. They may work with plants and animals; their tissues, cells, and products; and with yeast and bacteria.

Biochemists in industry generally work a 40-hour week, although they, like their counterparts in research, often put in many extra hours. They must be ready to spend a considerable amount of time keeping up with current literature, for example. Many biochemists occasionally travel to attend meetings or conferences. Those in research write papers for presentation at meetings or for publication in scientific journals.

Individuals interested in biochemistry must have the patience to work for long periods on a project without necessarily getting the desired results. Biochemistry is often a team affair, requiring an ability to work well and cooperate with others. Successful biochemists are continually learning and increasing their skills.

OUTLOOK

Employment for biological scientists, including biochemists, is expected to grow about as fast as the average for all occupations through 2014, according to the U.S. Department of Labor, as the number of trained scientists has increased faster than available funding. Competition will be strong for basic research positions, and candidates with more education and the experience it brings will be more likely to find the positions they want. Employment is available in health-related fields, where the emphasis is on finding cures for such diseases as cancer, muscular dystrophy, AIDS, and Alzheimer's. Additional jobs will be created to produce genetically engineered drugs and other products in the new and rapidly expanding field of genetic engineering. In this area, the outlook is best for biochemists with advanced degrees who can conduct genetic and cellular research. A caveat exists, however. Employment growth may slow somewhat as the number of new biotechnology firms slows and existing firms merge. Biochemists with bachelor's degrees who have difficulty entering their chosen career field may find openings as technicians or technologists or may choose to transfer their skills to other biological science fields.

It is estimated that over the next decade, 68 percent of those entering the workforce will be women and members of other minority groups. The federal government, recognizing this situation, offers a variety of special programs (through the National Science Foundation and the National Institutes of Health) to bring women, minorities, and persons with disabilities into the field.

FOR MORE INFORMATION

For a copy of Partnerships in Health Care, *a brochure discussing clinical laboratory careers, and other information, contact*
American Association for Clinical Chemistry
1850 K Street, NW, Suite 625
Washington, DC 20006-2213
Tel: 800-892-1400
http://www.aacc.org

For general information about chemistry careers and approved education programs, contact
American Chemical Society
1155 16th Street, NW
Washington, DC 20036-4801
Tel: 800-227-5558
http://www.chemistry.org

For information on careers in the biological sciences, contact
American Institute of Biological Sciences
1444 I Street, NW, Suite 200
Washington, DC 20005-6535

Tel: 202-628-1500
Email: admin@aibs.org
http://www.aibs.org

For information on educational programs, contact
American Society for Biochemistry and Molecular Biology
Education Information
9650 Rockville Pike
Bethesda, MD 20814-3996
Tel: 301-634-7145
Email: asbmb@asbmb.org
http://www.asbmb.org

For career resources, contact
American Society for Investigative Pathology
9650 Rockville Pike
Bethesda, MD 20814-3993
Tel: 301-634-7130
Email: asip@asip.org
http://www.asip.org

Chemical Engineers

OVERVIEW

Chemical engineers take chemistry out of the laboratory and into the real world. They are involved in evaluating methods and equipment for the mass production of chemicals and other materials requiring chemical processing. They also develop products from these materials, such as plastics, metals, gasoline, detergents, pharmaceuticals, and foodstuffs. They develop or improve safe, environmentally sound processes, determine the least costly production method, and formulate the material for easy use and safe, economic transportation. Approximately 31,000 chemical engineers work in the United States.

HISTORY

Chemical engineering, defined in its most general sense as applied chemistry, existed even in early civilizations. Ancient Greeks, for example, distilled alcoholic beverages, as did the Chinese, who by 800 B.C. had learned to distill alcohol from the fermentation of rice. Aristotle, a fourth-century B.C. Greek philosopher, wrote about a process for obtaining fresh water by evaporating and condensing water from the sea.

The foundations of modern chemical engineering were laid out during the Renaissance, when experimentation and the questioning of accepted scientific theories became widespread. This period saw the development of many new chemical processes, such as those for producing sulfuric acid (for fertilizers and textile treatment) and alkalies (for soap). The atomic theories of John Dalton and Amedeo Avogadro, developed in the 1800s, supplied the theoretical underpinning for modern chemistry and chemical engineering.

With the advent of large-scale manufacturing in the mid-19th century, modern chemical engineering began to take shape. Chemical manufacturers were soon required to seek out chemists familiar with manufacturing processes. These early chemical engineers were called chemical technicians or industrial chemists. The first course in chemical engineering was taught in 1888 at the Massachusetts Institute of Technology, and by 1900, "chemical engineer" had become a widely used job title.

Chemical engineers are employed in increasing numbers to design new and more efficient ways to produce chemicals and chemical by-products. In the United States, they have been especially important in the development of petroleum-based fuels for internal combustion engine–powered vehicles. Their achievements range from the large-scale production of plastics, antibiotics, and synthetic rubbers to the development of high-octane gasoline.

THE JOB

Chemical engineering is one of the four major engineering disciplines (the others are electrical, mechanical, and civil). Because chemical engineers are rigorously trained not only in chemistry but also in physics, mathematics, and other sciences such as biology or geology, they are among the most versatile of all engineers, with many specialties, and they are employed in many industries. Chemical industries, which transform raw materials into desired products, employ the largest number of chemical engineers.

There are many stages in the production of chemicals and related materials, and the following paragraphs describe specific jobs responsibilities by production stage for chemical engineers. At smaller companies, engineers may have a hand in all of these production phases, while job duties are more specialized in larger plants.

Research engineers work with chemists to develop new processes and products, or they may develop better methods to make existing products. Product ideas may originate with the company's marketing department; with a chemist, chemical engineer, or other specialist; or with a customer. The basic chemical process for the product is then developed in a laboratory, where various experiments are conducted to determine the process's viability. Some projects die here.

Others go on to be developed and refined at pilot plants, which are small-scale versions of commercial plants. Chemical engineers in these plants run tests on the processes and make any necessary

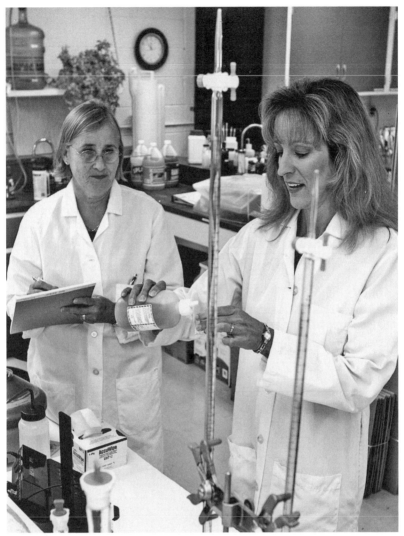

Chemists discuss a project in a laboratory. *(Jim West, The Image Works)*

modifications. They strive to improve the process, reduce safety hazards and waste, and cut production time and costs. Throughout the development stage, engineers keep detailed records of the proceedings, and they may abandon projects that aren't viable.

When a new process is judged to be viable, *process design engineers* determine how the product can most efficiently be produced on a large scale while still guaranteeing a consistently high-quality result. These engineers consider process requirements and cost, convenience and safety for the operators, waste minimization, legal regulations, and preservation of the environment. Besides working on the steps of the process, they also work on the design of the equipment to be used in the process. These chemical engineers are often assisted in plant and equipment design by mechanical, electrical, and civil engineers.

Project engineers oversee the construction of new plants and installation of new equipment. In construction, chemical engineers may work as *field engineers,* who are involved in the testing and initial operation of the equipment and assist in plant start-up and operator training. Once a process is fully implemented at a manufacturing plant, *production engineers* supervise the day-to-day operations. They are responsible for the rate of production, scheduling, worker safety, quality control, and other important operational concerns.

Chemical engineers working in environmental control are involved in waste management, recycling, and control of air and water pollution. They work with the engineers in research and development, process design, equipment and plant construction, and production to incorporate environmental protection measures into all stages of the chemical engineering process.

As *technical sales engineers,* chemical engineers may work with customers of manufactured products to determine what best fits their needs. They answer questions such as, "Could our products be used more economically than those now in use? Why does this paint peel?" and so on. Others work as managers, making policy and business decisions and overseeing the training of new personnel. The variety of job descriptions is almost limitless because of chemical engineers' versatility and adaptability.

REQUIREMENTS

High School
High school students interested in chemical engineering should take all the mathematics and science courses their schools offer. These should include algebra, geometry, calculus, trigonometry, chemistry, physics, and biology. Computer science courses are also highly recommended. In addition, students should take four years of English, and a foreign language is valuable. To enhance their desirability, students should participate in high school science and engineering clubs and other extracurricular activities.

Postsecondary Training
A bachelor's degree in chemical engineering is the minimum educational requirement for entering the field. For some positions, an

M.S., an M.B.A., or a Ph.D. may be required. A Ph.D. may be essential for advancement in research, teaching, and administration.

For their college studies, students should attend a chemical engineering program approved by the Accreditation Board for Engineering and Technology and the American Institute of Chemical Engineers (AIChE). There are more than 150 accredited undergraduate programs in chemical engineering in the United States offering bachelor's degrees. Some engineering programs last five or six years; these often include work experience in industry.

As career plans develop, students should consult with advisors about special career paths in which they are interested. Those who want to teach or conduct research will need a graduate degree. There are approximately 140 accredited chemical engineering graduate programs in the United States. A master's degree generally takes two years of study beyond undergraduate school, while a Ph.D. program requires four to six years.

In graduate school, students specialize in one aspect of chemical engineering, such as chemical kinetics or biotechnology. Graduate education also helps to obtain promotions, and some companies offer tuition reimbursement to encourage employees to take graduate courses. For engineers who would like to become managers, a master's degree in business administration may be helpful. Chemical engineers must be prepared for a lifetime of education to keep up with the rapid advances in technology.

Certification or Licensing
Chemical engineers must be licensed as professional engineers if their work involves providing services directly to the public. All 50 states and the District of Columbia have specific licensing requirements, which include graduation from an accredited engineering school, passing a written exam, and having at least four years of engineering experience. About one-third of all chemical engineers are licensed; they are called registered engineers. For more information on licensing and examination requirements, visit http://www.ncees.org.

Other Requirements
Important personal qualities are honesty, accuracy, objectivity, and perseverance. In addition, chemical engineers must be inquisitive, open-minded, creative, and flexible. Problem-solving ability is essential. To remain competitive in the job market, they should display initiative and leadership skills, exhibit the ability to work well in teams and collaborate across disciplines, and be able to work with people of different linguistic and cultural backgrounds.

EXPLORING

High school students should join science clubs and take part in other extracurricular activities and join such organizations as the Junior Engineering Technical Society (JETS). JETS participants have opportunities to enter engineering design and problem-solving contests and to learn team development skills. Science contests are also a good way to apply principles learned in classes to a special project. Students can also subscribe to the American Chemical Society's *Chem Matters*, a quarterly magazine for high school chemistry students.

College students can join professional associations, such as the American Chemical Society (ACS), AIChE, and the Society of Manufacturing Engineers (composed of individual associations with specific fields of interest), as student affiliates. Membership benefits include subscription to magazines—some of them geared specifically toward students—that provide the latest industry information. College students can also contact ACS or AIChE local sections to arrange to talk with some chemical engineers about what they do. These associations can also help them find summer or co-op work experiences.

In addition, the Society of Women Engineers (SWE) has a mentor program in which high school and college women are matched with an SWE member in their area. This member is available to answer questions and provide a firsthand introduction to a career in engineering.

EMPLOYERS

There are approximately 31,000 chemical engineers working in the United States. While many chemical engineers work in manufacturing industries, others are employed by federal and state governments, colleges and universities, and research and testing services. The list of individual employers, if cited, would take many pages. However, the following industry classifications indicate where most chemical engineers are employed: aerospace, fuels, electronics, food and consumer products, design and construction, materials, biotechnology, pharmaceuticals, environmental control, pulp and paper, public utilities, and consultation firms. Because of the nature of their training and background, chemical engineers can easily obtain employment with another company in a completely different field if necessary or desired.

STARTING OUT

Most chemical engineers obtain their first position through company recruiters sent to college campuses. Others may find employment with companies with whom they have had summer or work-study arrangements. Many respond to advertisements in professional journals or newspapers. The Internet now offers multiple opportunities to job seekers, and many libraries have programs that offer assistance in making use of the available job listings. Chemical engineers may also contact colleges and universities regarding positions as part-time teaching or laboratory assistants if they wish to continue study for a graduate degree. Student members of professional societies often use the employment services of these organizations, including resume data banks, online job listings, national employment clearinghouses, and employers' mailing lists.

Typically, new recruits begin as trainees or process engineers. They often begin work under the supervision of seasoned engineers. Many participate in special training programs designed to orient them to company processes, procedures, policies, and products. This allows the company to determine where the new personnel may best fulfill their needs. After this training period, new employees often rotate positions to get an all-around experience in working for the company.

ADVANCEMENT

Entry-level personnel usually advance to project or production engineers after learning the ropes in product manufacturing. They may then be assigned to sales and marketing. A large percentage of engineers no longer do engineering work by the tenth year of their employment. At that point, they often advance to supervisory or management positions. An M.B.A. enhances their opportunities for promotion. A doctoral degree is essential for university teaching or supervisory research positions. Some engineers may decide at this point that they prefer to start their own consulting firms. Continued advancement, raises, and increased responsibility are not automatic but depend on sustained demonstration of leadership skills.

EARNINGS

Though starting salaries have dipped somewhat in recent years, chemical engineering is still one of the highest paid scientific professions. Salaries vary with education, experience, industry, and employer. The U.S. Department of Labor reports that the median annual salary for chemical engineers was $78,860 in 2006. The lowest paid 10 percent earned less than $50,060; the highest paid 10 percent earned more than $118,670 annually. According to a 2005 salary survey by the National Association of Colleges and

Employers, starting annual salaries for those with bachelor's degrees in chemical engineering averaged $53,813; with master's degrees, $57,260; and Ph.D.'s, $79,591. Chemical engineers with doctoral degrees and many years of experience in supervisory and management positions may have salaries exceeding $100,000 annually.

Benefits offered depend on the employer; however, chemical engineers typically receive such things as paid vacation and sick days, health insurance, and retirement plans.

WORK ENVIRONMENT

Because the industries in which chemical engineers work are so varied—from academia to waste treatment and disposal—the working conditions also vary. Most chemical engineers work in clean, well-maintained offices, laboratories, or plants, although some occasionally work outdoors, particularly construction engineers. Travel to new or existing plants may be required. Some chemical engineers work with dangerous chemicals, but the adoption of safe working practices has greatly reduced potential health hazards. Chemical engineers at institutions of higher learning spend their time in classrooms or research laboratories.

The workweek for a chemical engineer in manufacturing is usually 40 hours, although many work longer hours. Because plants often operate around the clock, they may work different shifts or have irregular hours.

OUTLOOK

The U.S. Department of Labor projects that employment for chemical engineers will grow about as fast as the average for all occupations through 2014. Certain areas of the field will offer more job opportunities than others. Chemical and pharmaceutical companies, for example, will need engineers in research and development to work on new chemicals and more efficient processes. Additionally, growth will come in service industries, such as companies providing research and testing services. Job opportunities will be best in the energy, biotechnology, and nanotechnology segments of this industry sector.

FOR MORE INFORMATION

For information on undergraduate internships, summer jobs, and co-op programs, contact
American Chemical Society
1155 16th Street, NW

Washington, DC 20036-4801
Tel: 800-227-5558
Email: help@acs.org
http://www.chemistry.org

The American Chemistry Council offers useful information about the chemical industry, and maintains an informative Web site.
American Chemistry Council
1300 Wilson Boulevard
Arlington, VA 22209-2323
Tel: 703-741-5000
http://www.americanchemistry.com

For information on awards, accredited programs, internships, student chapters, and career opportunities, contact
American Institute of Chemical Engineers
3 Park Avenue
New York, NY 10016-5991
Tel: 800-242-4363
http://www.aiche.org

For information about programs, products, and a chemical engineering career brochure, contact
Junior Engineering Technical Society
1420 King Street, Suite 405
Alexandria, VA 22314-2750
Tel: 703-548-5387
Email: info@jets.org
http://www.jets.org

For information on National Engineers Week Programs held in many U.S. locations, contact
National Engineers Week Headquarters
1420 King Street
Alexandria, VA 22314-2750
Tel: 703-684-2852
Email: eweek@nspe.org
http://www.eweek.org

For information on training programs, seminars, and how to become a student member, contact
Society of Manufacturing Engineers
One SME Drive
Dearborn, MI 48121-2408

Tel: 800-733-4763
Email: careermentor@sme.org
http://www.sme.org

For information on career guidance literature, scholarships, and mentor programs, contact
Society of Women Engineers
230 East Ohio Street, Suite 400
Chicago, IL 60611-3265
Tel: 312-596-5223
Email: hq@swe.org
http://www.swe.org

─────── INTERVIEW ───────

Laura Ambrose is a chemical engineer at The Dow Chemical Company. She discussed her career with the editors of Careers in Focus: Chemistry.

Q. What is your job title? Where do you work?
A. My job title is global business manufacturing leader for polyols, polyglycols, and surfactants. I work in Freeport, Texas. I am responsible for leading the manufacturing organizations for two global business units, including 23 plants located in 13 countries. I'm responsible for about 500 people worldwide, and accountable for the environmental, health, safety, cost, operating reliability, employee satisfaction, product consistency, and customer loyalty for all plants and their products. I represent manufacturing and engineering on two global business teams with the polyurethanes and specialty chemical businesses where we prioritize and approve more than $100 million annually to optimize our global asset base and ensure the most effective operation.

Q. What do you like most about your job?
A. What I like most is being able to see the impact of my work on measurable results. I like seeing our business grow with new product offerings for consumers. I enjoy helping people in the company match their talents against job requirements and watching them grow in their career development.

Q. What do you find most challenging about your job?
A. What I find most challenging is that I have higher quality expectations of my work than I am sometimes able to fulfill. Sometimes daily time constraints limit the time I have to complete all

the tasks I need to handle, especially when my responsibilities stretch across home, family, and work commitments.

Q. Why did you decide to become a chemical engineer?

A. In high school, I was good at math and chemistry, and I loved technical subjects. My dad was an engineer, so it was easy to choose engineering as my degree. In college, I joined a cooperative education program, where a student alternates going to school and working in industry every other semester. It was during one of my co-op assignments that I discovered that I loved the fast pace and the challenge of the manufacturing environment. I have spent 20 years of my 25-year career in plant management roles.

Q. What type of educational path did you pursue to become a chemical engineer?

A. I have a bachelor of science in chemical engineering from Iowa State University. Iowa State offers an alternating cooperative education program where students can experience working in industry during their school curriculum. This allows students to try out different career options before they graduate. It takes a year longer to graduate, but the advantage of knowing the kind of work you enjoy far outweighs the extra school year.

Q. What are the most important professional qualities for chemical engineers?

A. I think the most important professional qualities for a chemical engineer are the same as for any other profession. You need to be able to learn quickly, because the world is continuously changing and work demands change frequently. You need to be able to demonstrate the ability to get results even under difficult conditions. You need to be resilient under pressure. And you need to be able to network with a large and diverse population in the workforce.

Q. What advice would you give to high school students who are interested in this career?

A. High school and college students should get involved in as many different kinds of sports, clubs, and classes as they can to discover for themselves what they are good at, and what they enjoy. This will help them choose a career that aligns their personal values with their work environment. If a student is interested in chemical engineering, they should talk to someone who is currently practicing this profession, or ask to shadow them for a day to see what a typical day is like. They could also visit career fairs, typically offered to high school and college students, and talk to companies that hire chemical engineers. They can also use Google [and other search engines] and check out what information is available online. Most companies have job links that describe their company and the jobs available.

Chemical Technicians

OVERVIEW

Chemical technicians assist chemists and chemical engineers in the research, development, testing, and manufacturing of chemicals and chemical-based products. Approximately 62,000 chemical technicians work in the United States.

HISTORY

The practice of modern chemistry goes back thousands of years to the earliest days when humans extracted medicinal substances from plants and shaped metals into tools and utensils for daily life. In the late 18th century, chemistry became established as a science when Antoine Lavoisier formulated the law of the conservation of matter. From that time until the present, the number and types of products attributed to the development and expansion of chemistry are almost incalculable.

The period following World War I was a time of enormous expansion of chemical technology and its application to the production of goods and consumer products such as high octane gasoline, antifreeze, pesticides, pharmaceuticals, plastics, and artificial fibers and fabrics. This rapid expansion increased the need for professionally trained chemists and technicians. The technicians, with their basic chemical knowledge and manual skills, were able to handle the tasks that did not require the specialized education of their bosses. These nonprofessionals sometimes had the title of junior chemist.

During the last 30 years, however, there has been a radical change in the status of the chemical technician from a "mere" assistant to a core professional. Automation and computerization have increased laboratory efficiency, and corporate downsizing has eliminated many

QUICK FACTS

School Subjects
Chemistry
Mathematics

Personal Skills
Following instructions
Technical/scientific

Work Environment
Primarily indoors
Primarily one location

Minimum Education Level
Some postsecondary training

Salary Range
$24,560 to $39,240 to
$60,120+

Certification or Licensing
None available

Outlook
More slowly than the average

DOT
022

GOE
02.05.01

NOC
2211

O*NET-SOC
19-4031.00

layers of intermediate hierarchy. The result has been to increase the level of responsibility and independence, meaning greater recognition of the importance of today's highly skilled and trained chemical technicians.

THE JOB

Most chemical technicians who work in the chemical industry are involved in the development, testing, and manufacturing of plastics, paints, detergents, synthetic fibers, industrial chemicals, and pharmaceuticals. Others work in the petroleum, aerospace, metals, electronics, automotive, and construction industries. Some chemical technicians work in universities and government laboratories.

They may work in any of the fields of chemistry, such as analytical, biochemistry, inorganic, organic, physical, or any of the many sub-branches of chemistry. Chemical engineering, which is a combination of chemistry and engineering, develops or improves manufacturing processes for making commercial amounts of chemicals, many of which were previously produced only in small quantities in laboratory glassware or a pilot plant.

Within these subfields, chemical technicians work in research and development, design and production, and quality control. In research and development, chemical laboratory technicians often work with Ph.D. chemists and chemical engineers to set up and monitor laboratory equipment and instruments, prepare laboratory setups, and record data.

Technicians often determine the chemical composition, concentration, stability, and level of purity on a wide range of materials. These may include ores, minerals, pollutants, foods, drugs, plastics, dyes, paints, detergents, chemicals, paper, and petroleum products. Although chemists or chemical engineers may design an experiment, technicians help them create process designs, develop written procedures, or devise computer simulations. They also select all necessary glassware, reagents, chemicals, and equipment. Technicians also perform analyses and report test results.

In the design and production area, chemical technicians work closely with chemical engineers to monitor the large-scale production of compounds and to help develop and improve the processes and equipment used. They prepare tables, charts, sketches, diagrams, and flowcharts that record and summarize the collected data. They work with pipelines, valves, pumps, and metal and glass tanks. Chemical technicians often use their input to answer manufacturing questions, such as how to transfer materials from one point to another, and to build, install, modify, and maintain processing equipment. They

Books to Read

Brown, Theodore E., H. Eugene LeMay, and Bruce E. Bursten. *Chemistry: The Central Science*. 10th ed. Upper Saddle River, N.J.: Prentice Hall, 2005.

Cobb, Cathy, and Monty L. Fetterolf. *The Joy of Chemistry: The Amazing Science of Familiar Things*. Amherst, N.Y.: Prometheus Books, 2005.

Davis, Raymond E., Regina Frey, Mickey Sarquis, and Jerry L. Sarquis. *Modern Chemistry*. Austin, Tex.: Holt Rinehart and Winston, 2005.

Gonick, Larry, and Craig Criddle. *The Cartoon Guide to Chemistry*. New York: Collins, 2005.

Guch, Ian. *The Complete Idiot's Guide to Chemistry*. 2d ed. New York: Alpha, 2006.

Karty, Joel. *The Nuts and Bolts of Organic Chemistry: A Student's Guide to Success*. Upper Saddle River, N.J.: Prentice Hall, 2005.

Princeton Review. *Cracking the SAT Chemistry Subject Test, 2007–2008 Edition*. New York: Princeton Review, 2007.

Schwarcz, Joe. *Radar, Hula Hoops, and Playful Pigs: 67 Digestible Commentaries on the Fascinating Chemistry of Everyday Life*. New York: Owl Books, 2001.

Timberlake, Karen C. *Chemistry: Study Guide and Selected Solutions: An Introduction to General, Organic, and Biological Chemistry*. 9th ed. San Francisco: Benjamin-Cummings Publishing Company, 2005.

Wilbraham, Anthony C., Dennis D. Staley, Michael S. Matta, and Edward L. Waterman. *Prentice Hall Chemistry*. Upper Saddle River, N.J.: Pearson Prentice Hall, 2007.

Woodburn, John H., and John Hazlett. *Opportunities in Chemistry Careers*. 2d ed. New York: McGraw-Hill, 2002.

also train and supervise production operators. They may operate small-scale equipment for determining process parameters.

Fuel technicians determine viscosities of oils and fuels, measure flash points (the temperature at which fuels catch fire), pour points (the coldest temperature at which the fuel can flow), and the heat output of fuels.

Pilot plant operators make erosion and corrosion tests on new construction materials to determine their suitability. They prepare chemicals for field testing and report on the effectiveness of new design concepts.

Applied research technicians help design new manufacturing or research equipment.

REQUIREMENTS

High School

You should take several years of science and mathematics in high school, and computer training is also important. While a minority of employers still hire high school graduates and place them into their own training programs, the majority prefer to hire graduates of community colleges who have completed two-year chemical technician programs or even bachelor degree recipients. If you plan on attending a four-year college, take as much as three years of high school mathematics, including algebra, geometry, and trigonometry; three years of physical sciences, including chemistry; and four years of English.

Postsecondary Training

Graduates of community college programs are productive much sooner than untrained individuals because they have the technical knowledge, laboratory experience, and skills for the job. Computer courses are necessary, as computers and computer-interfaced equipment are routinely used in the field. Realizing that many students become aware of technical career possibilities too late to satisfy college requirements, many community and technical colleges that offer chemical technician programs may also have noncredit courses that allow students to meet college entrance requirements.

Approximately 40 two-year colleges in the United States have chemical technology programs. Once enrolled in a two-year college program designed for chemical technicians, students should expect to take a number of chemistry courses with strong emphasis on laboratory work and the presentation of data. These courses include basic concepts of modern chemistry, such as atomic structure, descriptive chemistry of both organic and inorganic substances, analytical methods including quantitative and instrumental analysis, and physical properties of substances. Other courses include communications, physics, mathematics, industrial safety, and organic laboratory equipment and procedures.

Other Requirements

Besides the educational requirements, certain personal characteristics are necessary for successful chemical technicians. You must have both the ability and the desire to use mental and manual skills. You should also have a good supply of patience because experiments must frequently be repeated several times. You should be precise and like doing detailed work. Mechanical aptitude and good powers of observation are also needed. You should be able to follow directions closely and enjoy solving problems. Chemical technicians also need excellent organizational and communication skills. Other important qualities are a desire to learn new skills and a willingness to accept responsibility. In addition, you should have good eyesight, color perception, and hand-eye coordination.

EXPLORING

You can explore this field by joining high school science clubs or organizations and taking part in extracurricular activities such as the Junior Engineering Technical Society (JETS). Science contests are a good way to apply principles learned in classes to a special project. You can also subscribe to the American Chemical Society (ACS's) *ChemMatters,* a quarterly magazine for students taking chemistry in high school. Examples of topics covered in the magazine include the chemistry of lipstick, suntan products, contact lenses, and carbon-14 dating. Also, qualifying students can participate in Project SEED (Summer Education Experience for the Disadvantaged), a summer program designed to provide high school students from economically disadvantaged homes with the opportunity to experience science research in a laboratory environment. (Visit http://www.chemistry.org for more information.)

Once you are in college, you can join the student affiliates of professional associations such as the ACS and the American Institute of Chemical Engineers (AIChE). Membership allows students to experience the professionalism of a career in chemistry. You can also contact ACS or AIChE local sections to talk with chemists and chemical engineers about what they do. These associations may also help students find summer or co-op work experiences.

EMPLOYERS

Almost all chemical laboratories, no matter their size or function, employ chemical technicians to assist their chemists or chemical engineers with research as well as routine laboratory work. Therefore, chemical technicians can find employment wherever chemistry is involved: in industrial laboratories, in government agencies such as the Department of Health and Human Services and the Department of Agriculture, and at colleges and universities. They can work in almost any field of chemical activity, such as industrial manufacturing of all kinds, pharmaceuticals, food, and production of chemicals. There are approximately 62,000 chemical technicians employed in the United States.

Mean Annual Earnings by Specialty, 2006

Electric power generation, transmission and distribution	$58,280
Petroleum and coal products manufacturing	$48,040
Resin, synthetic rubber, and artificial synthetic	$46,390
Basic chemical manufacturing	$46,040
Scientific research and development services	$42,640
Pharmaceutical and medicine manufacturing	$41,740
Architectural, engineering, and related services	$32,980

Source: U.S. Department of Labor

STARTING OUT

Graduates of chemical technology programs often find jobs during the last term of their two-year programs. Some companies work with local community colleges and technical schools to maintain a supply of trained chemical technicians. Recruiters regularly visit most colleges where chemical technology programs are offered. Most employers recruit locally or regionally. Because companies hire locally and work closely with technical schools, career services offices are usually successful in finding jobs for their graduates.

Some recruiters also go to four-year colleges and look for chemists with bachelor's degrees. Whether a company hires bachelor's-level chemists or two-year chemical technology graduates depends on both the outlook of the company and the local supply of graduates.

Internships and co-op work are highly regarded by employers, and participation in such programs is a good way to get your foot in the door. Many two- and four-year schools have co-op programs in which full-time students work approximately 20 hours a week for a local company. Such programs may be available to high school seniors as well. Students in these programs develop a good knowledge of the employment possibilities and frequently stay with their co-op employers.

More and more companies are using contract workers to perform technicians' jobs, and this is another way to enter the field. There are local agencies that place technicians with companies for special projects or temporary assignments that last anywhere from a month to a year or more. Many of these contract workers are later hired on a full-time basis.

ADVANCEMENT

Competent chemical technicians can expect to have long-term career paths. Top research and development positions are open to technically trained people, whether they start out with an associate's degree in chemical technology, a bachelor's degree in chemistry, or just a lot of valuable experience with no degree. There are also opportunities for advancement in the areas of technology development and technology management, providing comparable pay for these separate but equal paths. Some companies have the same career path for all technicians, regardless of education level. Other companies have different career ladders for technicians and chemists but will promote qualified technicians to chemists and move them up that path.

Some companies may require additional formal schooling for promotion, and the associate's degree can be a stepping-stone toward a bachelor's degree in chemistry. Many companies encourage their technicians to continue their education, and most reimburse tuition costs. Continuing education in the form of seminars, workshops, and in-company presentations is also important for advancement. Chemical technicians who want to advance must keep up with current developments in the field by reading trade and technical journals and publications.

EARNINGS

Earnings for chemical technicians vary based on their education, experience, employer, and location. The U.S. Department of Labor reports the median hourly wage for chemical technicians as $18.87 in 2006. A technician making this wage and working full-time would earn a yearly salary of approximately $39,240. The top 10 percent earned $28.90 per hour (or $60,120 annually) or more in 2006, while the lowest 10 percent earned $11.81 an hour (or $24,560 annually). Salaries tend to be highest in private industry and lowest in colleges and universities.

If a technician belongs to a union, his or her wages and benefits depend on the union agreement. However, the percentage of technicians who belong to a union is very small. Benefits depend on the employer, but they usually include paid vacations and holidays, insurance, and tuition refund plans. Technicians normally work a five-day, 40-hour week. Occasional overtime may be necessary.

WORK ENVIRONMENT

The chemical industry is one of the safest industries in which to work. Laboratories and plants normally have safety committees and safety engineers who closely monitor equipment and practices to minimize hazards. Chemical technicians usually receive safety training both in school and at work to recognize potential hazards and to take appropriate measures.

Most chemical laboratories are clean and well lighted. Technicians often work at tables and benches while operating laboratory equipment and are usually provided office or desk space to record data and prepare reports. The work can sometimes be monotonous and repetitive, as when making samples or doing repetitive testing. Chemical plants are usually clean, and the number of operating personnel for the space involved is often very low.

OUTLOOK

The U.S. Department of Labor expects employment for chemical technicians to grow more slowly than the average for all occupations through 2014. Despite this prediction, chemical technicians will be in demand as the chemical and pharmaceutical industries work to improve and produce new medicines and personal care products. Chemical technicians will also be needed by businesses that provide environmental services and "earth-friendly" products, analytical development and services, custom or niche products and services, and quality control.

Graduates of chemical technology programs will continue to face competition from bachelor's-level chemists. The chemical and chemical-related industries will continue to become increasingly sophisticated in both their products and their manufacturing techniques. Technicians trained to deal with automation and complex production methods will have the best employment opportunities.

FOR MORE INFORMATION

For general career information, as well as listings of chemical technology programs, internships, and summer job opportunities, contact
American Chemical Society
1155 16th Street, NW
Washington, DC 20036-4801
Tel: 800-227-5558
http://www.chemistry.org

The American Chemistry Council offers a great deal of information about the chemical industry, and maintains an informative Web site.

American Chemistry Council
1300 Wilson Boulevard
Arlington, VA 22209-2323
Tel: 703-741-5000
http://www.americanchemistry.com

For information on awards, student chapters, and career opportunities, contact

American Institute of Chemical Engineers
3 Park Avenue
New York, NY 10016-5991
Tel: 800-242-4363
http://www.aiche.org

For information about programs, products, and a chemical engineering career brochure, contact

Junior Engineering Technical Society
1420 King Street, Suite 405
Alexandria, VA 22314-2750
Tel: 703-548-5387
Email: info@jets.org
http://www.jets.org

For fun and educational information on the field of chemistry, check out the following Web site:

Rader's CHEM4KIDS!
http://www.chem4kids.com

Chemists

QUICK FACTS

School Subjects
Chemistry
Mathematics

Personal Skills
Communication/ideas
Technical/scientific

Work Environment
Primarily indoors
Primarily one location

Minimum Education Level
Bachelor's degree

Salary Range
$35,480 to $59,870 to
$106,310+

Certification or Licensing
None available

Outlook
More slowly than the average

DOT
022

GOE
02.02.01

NOC
2112

O*NET-SOC
19-2031.00

OVERVIEW

Chemists are scientists who study the composition, changes, reactions, and transformations of matter. They may specialize in analytical, biological, inorganic, organic, or physical chemistry. They may work in laboratories, hospitals, private companies, government agencies, or colleges and universities. Approximately 90,000 chemists are employed in the United States.

HISTORY

The ancient Egyptians began gathering knowledge about matter and organizing it into systems, developing what is now known as alchemy, which mixed science with metaphysics. This was the beginning of chemistry. Alchemists concentrated their efforts on trying to convert lead and other common metals into gold. Alchemy dominated the European chemical scene until modern chemistry started to replace it in the 18th century.

In the late 1700s, Antoine Lavoisier discovered that the weight of the products of a chemical reaction always equaled the combined weight of the original reactants. This discovery became known as the law of the conservation of matter. In the 1800s, the work of scientists such as John Dalton, Humphrey Davy, Michael Faraday, Amedeo Avogadro, Dmitri Mendeleyev, and Julius Meyer laid the foundations for modern chemistry. The latter two men independently established the periodic law and periodic table of elements, making chemistry a rational, predictable science. The technological advances of the industrial revolution provided both the necessity and the incentive to get rid of alchemy and make chemistry the science it is today.

THE JOB

Many chemists work in research and development laboratories. However, some chemists spend most of their time in offices or libraries, where they do academic research on new developments or write reports on research results. Often these chemists determine the need for certain products and tell the researchers what experiments or studies to pursue in the laboratory.

Chemists who work in research are usually focused on either basic or applied research. Basic research entails searching for new knowledge about chemicals and chemical properties. This helps scientists broaden their understanding of the chemical world, and often these new discoveries appear later as applied research. Chemists who do applied research use the knowledge obtained from basic research to create new and/or better products that may be used by consumers or in manufacturing processes, such as the development of new pharmaceuticals for the treatment of a specific disease or superior plastics for space travel. In addition, they may hold marketing or sales positions, advising customers about how to use certain products. These jobs are especially important in the field of agriculture, where customers need to know the safe and effective doses of pesticides to use to protect workers, consumers, and the environment. Chemists who work in marketing and sales must understand the scientific terminology involved so they can translate it into nontechnical terms for the customer.

Some chemists work in quality control and production in manufacturing plants. They work with plant engineers to establish manufacturing processes for specific products and to ensure that the chemicals are safely and effectively handled within the plant.

Chemists also work as instructors in high schools, colleges, and universities. Many at the university level are also involved in basic or applied research. In fact, most of America's basic research is conducted in a university setting.

There are many branches of chemistry, each with a different set of requirements. A chemist may go into basic or applied research, marketing, teaching, or a variety of other related positions. *Analytical chemists* study the composition and nature of rocks, soils, and other substances and develop procedures for analyzing them. They also identify the presence of pollutants in soil, water, and air. *Biological chemists,* also known as *biochemists,* study the composition and actions of complex chemicals in living organisms. They identify and analyze the chemical processes related to biological functions, such as metabolism or reproduction, and they are often involved directly in genetics studies. They are also employed in the pharmaceutical and food industries.

The distinction between organic and inorganic chemistry is based on carbon-hydrogen compounds. Ninety-nine percent of all chemicals that occur naturally contain carbon. *Organic chemists* study the chemical compounds that contain carbon and hydrogen, while *inorganic chemists* study all other substances. *Physical chemists* study the physical characteristics of atoms and molecules. A physical chemist working in a nuclear power plant, for example, may study the properties of the radioactive materials involved in the production of electricity derived from nuclear fission reactions.

Because chemistry is such a diverse field, central to every reaction and the transformation of all matter, it is necessary for chemists to specialize in specific areas. Still, each field covers a wide range of work and presents almost limitless possibilities for experimentation and study. Often, chemists will team up with colleagues in other specialties to seek solutions to their common problems.

REQUIREMENTS

High School

If you are interested in a chemistry career, begin preparing yourself in high school by taking advanced-level courses in the physical sciences, mathematics, and English. A year each of physics, chemistry, and biology is essential, as are the abilities to read graphs and charts, perform difficult mathematical calculations, and write scientific reports. Computer science courses are also important to take, since much of your documentation and other work will involve using computers.

Postsecondary Training

The minimum educational requirement for a chemist is a bachelor's degree in science. However, in the upper levels of basic and applied research, and especially in a university setting, most positions are filled by people with doctoral degrees.

More than 630 bachelor's, 300 master's, and 190 doctoral degree programs are accredited by the American Chemical Society (ACS). Many colleges and universities also offer advanced degree programs in chemistry. Upon entering college, students majoring in chemistry should expect to take classes in several branches of the field, such as organic, inorganic, analytical, physical chemistry, and biochemistry. Chemistry majors must advance their skills in mathematics, physics, and biology and be proficient with computers.

Survey Says

In 2005, the American Chemical Society surveyed its members regarding employment and workplace issues. Noteworthy results include:

- Male members earned median salaries of $88,000, while female members earned median salaries of $68,000 annually.
- Nearly 52 percent of member-chemists worked in manufacturing, 27.4 percent worked in academia, 7.7 percent worked in government, and 1.6 percent were self-employed.
- Slightly more than 63 percent of members held a Ph.D.; 17 percent held a master's degree, and 19.9 percent held a bachelor's degree.

Other Requirements

Chemists must be detail-oriented, precise workers. They often work with minute quantities, taking minute measurements. They must record all details and reaction changes that may seem insignificant and unimportant to the untrained observer. They must keep careful records of their work and have the patience to repeat experiments over and over again, perhaps varying the conditions in only a small way each time. They should be inquisitive and have an interest in what makes things work and how things fit together. Chemists may work alone or in groups. A successful chemist is not only self-motivated but should be a team player and have good written and oral communication skills.

EXPLORING

The best means of exploring a career in chemistry while still in high school is to pay attention and work hard in chemistry class. This will give you the opportunity to learn the scientific method, perform chemical experiments, and become familiar with chemical terminology. Advanced placement (AP) courses will also help. Contact the department of chemistry at a local college or university to discuss the field and arrange tours of their laboratories or classrooms. Because of the extensive training involved, it is very unlikely that a high school student will be able to get a summer job or internship working in a laboratory. However, you may want to contact local manufacturers or research institutions to explore the possibility.

EMPLOYERS

About 43 percent of the approximately 90,000 chemists employed in the United States work for manufacturing companies. Most of these companies are involved in chemical manufacturing, producing such products as plastics, soaps, paints, drugs, and synthetic materials. Chemists are also needed in industrial manufacturing and pilot plant locations. Examples of large companies that employ many chemists are Dow Chemical, DuPont, Monsanto, and Campbell Soup Company.

Chemists also work for government agencies, such as the Department of Health and Human Services, the Department of Agriculture, the Department of Energy, and the National Institute of Standards and Technology. Chemists may find positions in laboratories at institutions of higher learning that are devoted to research. In addition, some chemists work in full-time teaching positions in high schools and universities.

STARTING OUT

Once you have a degree in chemistry, job opportunities will begin to become available. Summer jobs may become available after your sophomore or junior year of college. You can attend chemical trade fairs and science and engineering fairs to meet and perhaps interview prospective employers. Professors or faculty advisors may know of job openings, and you can begin breaking into the field by using these connections.

If you are a senior and are interested in pursuing an academic career at a college or university, you should apply to graduate schools. You will want to begin focusing even more on the specific type of chemistry you wish to practice and teach (for example, inorganic chemistry or analytical chemistry). Look for universities that have strong programs and eminent professors in your intended field of specialty. By getting involved with the basic research of a specific branch of chemistry while in graduate school, you can become a highly employable expert in your field.

ADVANCEMENT

In nonacademic careers, advancement usually takes the form of increased job responsibilities accompanied by salary increases. For example, a chemist may rise from doing basic research in a laboratory to being a group leader, overseeing and directing the work of others. Some chemists eventually leave the laboratory and set up their own consulting businesses, serving the needs of private manu-facturing companies or government agencies. Others may accept university faculty positions.

Chemists who work in a university setting follow the advancement procedures for that institution. Typically, a chemist in academia with a doctoral degree will go from instructor to assistant professor to associate professor and finally to full professor. To advance through these ranks, faculty members at most colleges and universities are expected to perform original research and publish their papers in scientific journals of chemistry and/or other sciences. As the rank of faculty members increases, so do their duties, salaries, responsibilities, and reputations.

EARNINGS

Salary levels for chemists vary based on education, experience, and the area in which they work. According to the U.S. Department of Labor, median annual earnings for all chemists in 2006 were $59,870. The lowest paid 10 percent earned less than $35,480, and the highest paid 10 percent made more than $106,310 annually. Chemists working for the federal government had mean incomes of $91,550 in 2006.

According to the ACS's salary survey of 2005, the median salary of its members with Ph.D.'s was $93,800; those with master's degrees, $75,000, and those with bachelor's degrees, $64,000. Salaries tend to be highest on the East Coast and West Coast. In addition, those working in industry usually have the highest earnings, while those in academia have the lowest.

As highly trained, full-time professionals, most chemists receive health insurance, paid vacations, and sick leave. The specifics of these benefits vary from employer to employer. Chemists who teach at the college or university level usually work on an academic calendar, which means they get extensive breaks from teaching classes during summer and winter recesses.

WORK ENVIRONMENT

Most chemists work in clean, well-lighted laboratories that are well organized and neatly kept. They may have their own offices and share laboratory space with other chemists. Some chemists work at such locations as oil wells or refineries, where their working conditions may be uncomfortable. Occasionally, chemical reactions or substances being tested may have strong odors. Other chemicals may be extremely dangerous to the touch, and chemists will have to wear protective devices such as goggles, gloves, and protective clothing and work in special, well-ventilated hoods.

OUTLOOK

The U.S. Department of Labor predicts that employment for chemists will grow more slowly than the average for all occupations through 2014. Employment opportunities will be best for researchers who are interested in working in pharmaceutical and medicine manufacturing and in professional, scientific, and technical services firms. Aspiring chemists will do well to get graduate degrees to maximize their opportunities for employment and advancement. The ACS reports that 53 percent of 2003–04 chemistry master's graduates found full-time permanent jobs (as compared to only 35 percent of bachelor's graduates).

Those wishing to teach full time at the university or college level should find opportunities but also stiff competition. Many of these institutions are choosing to hire people for adjunct faculty positions (part-time positions without benefits) instead of for full-time, tenure-track positions. Nevertheless, a well-trained chemist should have little trouble finding some type of employment.

FOR MORE INFORMATION

For a copy of Partnerships in Health Care, *a brochure discussing clinical laboratory careers, and other information, contact*
American Association for Clinical Chemistry
1850 K Street, NW, Suite 625
Washington, DC 20006-2213
Tel: 800-892-1400
http://www.aacc.org

For career and industry information, contact
American Association of Textile Chemists and Colorists
PO Box 12215
Research Triangle Park, NC 27709
Tel: 919-549-8141
http://www.aatcc.org

For general information about chemistry careers and approved education programs, contact
American Chemical Society
1155 16th Street, NW

Washington, DC 20036-4801
Tel: 800-227-5558
http://www.chemistry.org

The American Chemistry Council provides useful information about the chemical industry, and maintains an informative Web site.
American Chemistry Council
1300 Wilson Boulevard
Arlington, VA 22209-2323
Tel: 703-741-5000
http://www.americanchemistry.com

For information on careers in the cosmetics industry, contact
Society of Cosmetic Chemists
120 Wall Street, Suite 2400
New York, NY 10005-4088
Tel: 212-668-1500
http://www.scconline.org

To read about the important role women have played in chemistry, visit
Her Lab In Your Life: Women in Chemistry
http://www.chemheritage.org/women_chemistry

College Professors, Chemistry

QUICK FACTS

School Subjects
Chemistry
English
Speech

Personal Skills
Communication/ideas
Helping/teaching

Work Environment
Primarily indoors
Primarily one location

Minimum Education Level
Master's degree

Salary Range
$36,160 to $61,220 to
$116,910+

Certification or Licensing
None available

Outlook
Much faster than the average

DOT
090

GOE
12.03.02

NOC
4121

O*NET-SOC
25-1052.00

OVERVIEW

College chemistry professors instruct undergraduate and graduate students in chemistry and related subjects at colleges and universities. They are responsible for lecturing classes, supervising labs, and creating and grading examinations. They also may conduct research, write for publication, and aid in administration. Approximately 19,560 postsecondary chemistry teachers are employed in the United States.

HISTORY

The concept of colleges and universities goes back many centuries. These institutions evolved slowly from monastery schools, which trained a select few for certain professions, notably theology. The terms *college* and *university* have become virtually interchangeable in America outside the walls of academia, although originally they designated two very different kinds of institutions.

Two of the most notable early European universities were the University of Bologna in Italy and the University of Paris. The University of Bologna was thought to have been established in the 12th century and the University of Paris was chartered in 1201. These universities were considered to be models after which other European universities were patterned. Oxford University in England was probably established during the 12th century. Oxford served as a model for early American colleges and universities and today is still considered one of the world's leading institutions.

Harvard, the first U.S. college, was established in 1636. Its stated purpose was to train men for the ministry. All of the early colleges were established for religious training. With the growth of state-supported institutions in the early 18th century, the process of freeing the curriculum from ties with the church began. The University of Virginia established the first liberal arts curriculum in 1825, and these innovations were later adopted by many other colleges and universities.

Although the original colleges in the United States were patterned after Oxford University, they later came under the influence of German universities. During the 19th century, more than 9,000 Americans went to Germany to study. The emphasis in German universities was on the scientific method. Most of the people who had studied in Germany returned to the United States to teach in universities, bringing this objective, factual approach to education, the sciences (including chemistry, biology, and mathematics), and other fields of learning.

Benjamin Rush, a physician and one of the signers of the Declaration of Independence, is considered to be the first appointed professor of chemistry in the United States. In 1769, Rush began teaching at the College of Philadelphia (now the University of Pennsylvania), and published the first American textbook on chemistry.

Today, the American Chemical Society has approved more than 630 bachelor's, 300 master's, and 190 doctoral degree programs in chemistry. Some of the top chemistry programs in the United States can be found at the California Institute of Technology, the Massachusetts Institute of Technology, Stanford University, and the University of California–Berkeley.

THE JOB

College and university faculty members teach chemistry or related subjects at junior colleges or at four-year colleges and universities. At four-year institutions, most faculty members are *assistant professors, associate professors,* or *full professors.* These three types of professorships differ in regards to status, job responsibilities, and salary. Assistant professors are new faculty members who are working to get tenure (status as a permanent professor); they seek to advance to associate and then to full professorships.

College chemistry professors perform three main functions: teaching, advising, and research. Their most important responsibility is to teach students. Their role within a chemistry department will determine the level of courses they teach and the number of courses per semester. Most professors work with students at all levels, from college freshmen to graduate students. They may head several classes a semester or only a few a year. Some of their classes will have large enrollment, while graduate seminars may consist of only 12 or fewer students. Though college chemistry professors may spend fewer than 10 hours a week in the actual classroom, they spend many hours preparing lectures and lesson plans, grading papers and exams, and preparing grade reports. They also schedule office hours during the week to be available to students outside of the lecture hall, and they meet with students individually throughout the semester. Many professors teaching this discipline also work in the field as practicing chemists or chemical engineers.

In the classroom, chemistry professors teach classes on such topics as analytical chemistry, atmospheric chemistry, biochemistry, bioinorganic chemistry, biophysical chemistry, chemical biology, chemical engineering, chemical research, electrochemistry, environmental chemistry, inorganic chemistry, materials science, nuclear chemistry, organic chemistry, organometallic chemistry, pharmacology, physical chemistry, and polymer chemistry. They also administer exams and assign textbook reading and other research. In some courses, professors rely heavily on laboratories to transmit course material.

Another important responsibility is advising students. Not all chemistry professors serve as advisers, but those who do must set aside large blocks of time to guide students through the program. College chemistry professors who serve as advisers may have any number of students assigned to them, from fewer than 10 to more than 100, depending on the administrative policies of the college. Their responsibility may involve looking over a planned program of studies to make sure the students meet requirements for graduation, or it may involve working intensively with each student on many aspects of college life.

The third responsibility of chemistry professors is research and publication. Faculty members who are heavily involved in research programs sometimes are assigned a smaller teaching load. College chemistry professors publish their research findings in various scholarly journals, such as *Analytical Chemistry,* the *Journal of Physical Chemistry,* and the *Journal of Organic Chemistry.* They also write books based on their research or on their own knowledge and experience in the field. Most textbooks are written by college and university teachers.

Publishing a significant amount of work has been the traditional standard by which assistant chemistry professors prove themselves worthy of becoming permanent, tenured faculty. Typically, pressure to publish is greatest for assistant professors. Pressure to publish

A chemistry professor works with a student on an experiment. *(Marty Heitner, The Image Works)*

increases again if an associate professor wishes to be considered for a promotion to full professorship. Professors in junior colleges face less pressure to publish than those in four-year institutions.

Some faculty members eventually rise to the position of *chemistry department chair,* where they govern the affairs of the entire department. Department chairs, faculty, and other professional staff members are aided in their myriad duties by *graduate assistants,* who may help develop teaching materials, conduct research, give examinations, teach lower-level courses, and carry out other activities.

Some college chemistry professors may also conduct classes in an extension program. In such a program, they teach evening and weekend courses for the benefit of people who otherwise would not be able to take advantage of the institution's resources. They may travel away from the campus and meet with a group of students at another location. They may work full time for the extension division or may divide their time between on-campus and off-campus teaching.

Distance learning programs, an increasingly popular option for students, give chemistry professors the opportunity to use today's technologies to remain in one place while teaching students who are at a variety of locations simultaneously. The chemistry professor's duties, like those when teaching correspondence courses conducted by mail, include grading work that students send in at periodic intervals and advising students of their progress. Computers, the Internet, email, and video conferencing, however, are some of the technology tools that allow professors and students to communicate in "real time" in a virtual classroom setting. Meetings may be scheduled during the same time as traditional classes or during evenings and weekends. Professors who do this work are sometimes known as *extension work, correspondence,* or *distance learning instructors.* They may teach online courses in addition to other classes or may have distance learning as their major teaching responsibility.

The *junior college chemistry instructor* has many of the same kinds of responsibilities as does the chemistry professor in a four-year college or university. Because junior colleges offer only a two-year program, they teach only undergraduates.

REQUIREMENTS

High School
Your high school's college preparatory program likely includes courses in English, science (especially chemistry), foreign language, history, math, and government. In addition, you should take courses in speech to get a sense of what it will be like to lecture to a group of students. Your school's debate team can also help you develop public speaking skills, along with research skills.

Postsecondary Training
At least one advanced degree in chemistry or a related field is required to be a professor in a college or university. The master's degree is considered the minimum standard, and graduate work beyond the master's is usually desirable. If you hope to advance in academic rank above instructor, most institutions require a doctorate.

In the last year of your undergraduate program, you'll apply to graduate programs in chemistry. Standards for admission to a graduate program can be high and the competition heavy, depending on the school. Once accepted into a program, your responsibilities will be similar to those of your professors—in addition to attending seminars, you'll research, prepare articles for publication, and teach some undergraduate courses.

You may find employment in a junior college with only a master's degree. Advancement in responsibility and in salary, however, is more likely to come if you have earned a doctorate.

Other Requirements
You should enjoy reading, writing, and researching. Not only will you spend many years studying in school; your whole career will

be based on communicating your ideas. People skills are important because you'll be dealing directly with students, administrators, and other faculty members on a daily basis. You should feel comfortable in a role of authority and possess self-confidence.

EXPLORING

Your high school chemistry teachers use many of the same skills as college chemistry professors, so talk to your teachers about their careers and their college experiences. You can develop your own teaching experience by volunteering at a community center, working at a day care center, or working at a summer camp (especially one that focuses on science). Also, spend some time on a college campus to get a sense of the environment. Write to colleges for their admissions brochures and course catalogs (or check them out online); read about the faculty members in chemistry departments and the courses they teach. Before visiting college campuses, make arrangements to speak to professors who teach courses that interest you. These professors may allow you to sit in on their classes and observe. Also, make appointments with college advisers and with people in the admissions and recruitment offices. If your grades are good enough, you might be able to serve as a teaching assistant during your undergraduate years, which can give you experience leading discussions and grading papers.

EMPLOYERS

Approximately 19,560 postsecondary chemistry teachers are employed in the United States. Employment opportunities vary based on area of study and education. With a doctorate, a number of publications, and a record of good teaching, professors should find opportunities in universities all across the country. Chemistry professors teach in undergraduate and graduate programs. The teaching jobs at doctoral institutions are usually better paying and more prestigious. The most sought-after positions are those that offer tenure. Teachers that have only a master's degree will be limited to opportunities with junior colleges, community colleges, and some small private institutions.

STARTING OUT

You should start the process of finding a teaching position while you are in graduate school. The process includes developing a curriculum vitae (a detailed, academic resume), writing for publication, assisting with research, attending conferences, and gaining teaching experience and recommendations. Many students begin applying for teaching positions while finishing their graduate program. For most positions at four-year institutions, you must travel to large conferences where interviews can be arranged with representatives from the universities to which you have applied.

Because of the competition for tenure-track positions, you may have to work for a few years in temporary positions, visiting various schools as an adjunct professor. Some professional associations maintain lists of teaching opportunities in their areas. They may also make lists of applicants available to college administrators looking to fill an available position.

ADVANCEMENT

The normal pattern of advancement is from instructor to assistant professor, to associate professor, to full professor. All four academic ranks are concerned primarily with teaching and research. College faculty members who have an interest in and a talent for administration may be advanced to chair of a department or to dean of their college. A few become college or university presidents or other types of administrators.

The instructor is usually an inexperienced college teacher. He or she may hold a doctorate or may have completed all the Ph.D. requirements except for the dissertation. Most colleges look upon the rank of instructor as the period during which the college is trying out the teacher. Instructors usually are advanced to the position of assistant professors within three to four years. Assistant professors are given up to about six years to prove themselves worthy of tenure, and if they do so, they become associate professors. Some professors choose to remain at the associate level. Others strive to become full professors and receive greater status, salary, and responsibilities.

Most colleges have clearly defined promotion policies from rank to rank for faculty members, and many have written statements about the number of years in which instructors and assistant professors may remain in grade. Administrators in many colleges hope to encourage younger faculty members to increase their skills and competencies and thus to qualify for the more responsible positions of associate professor and full professor.

EARNINGS

Earnings vary by the departments professors work in, by the size of the school, by the type of school (public, private, women's only, for example), and by the level of position the professor holds.

According to the U.S. Department of Labor, in 2006, the median salary for postsecondary chemistry teachers was $61,220, with 10 percent earning $116,910 or more and 10 percent earning $36,160 or less. Chemistry teachers employed at junior colleges had mean annual earnings of $59,070. Those with the highest earnings tend to be senior tenured faculty; those with the lowest, graduate assistants. Professors working on the West Coast and the East Coast and those working at doctorate-granting institutions also tend to have the highest salaries. Many professors try to increase their earnings by completing research, publishing in their field, or teaching additional courses.

Benefits for full-time faculty typically include health insurance and retirement funds and, in some cases, stipends for travel related to research, housing allowances, and tuition waivers for dependents.

WORK ENVIRONMENT

A college or university is usually a pleasant place in which to work. Campuses bustle with all types of activities and events, stimulating ideas, and a young, energetic population. Much prestige comes with success as a professor and scholar; professors have the respect of students, colleagues, and others in their community.

Depending on the size of the department, college chemistry professors may have their own office, or they may have to share an office with one or more colleagues. Their department may provide them with a computer, Internet access, and research assistants. College professors are also able to do much of their office work at home. They can arrange their schedule around class hours, academic meetings, and the established office hours when they meet with students. Most college teachers work more than 40 hours each week. Although college professors may teach only two or three classes a semester, they spend many hours preparing for lectures, examining student work, and conducting research.

OUTLOOK

The U.S. Department of Labor predicts much faster than average employment growth for college and university professors through 2014. College enrollment is projected to grow due to an increased number of 18- to 24-year-olds, an increased number of adults returning to college, and an increased number of foreign-born students. Retirement of current faculty members will also provide job openings. However, competition for full-time, tenure-track positions at four-year schools will be very strong.

A number of factors threaten to change the way colleges and universities hire faculty. Some university leaders are developing more business-based methods of running their schools, focusing on profits and budgets. This can affect college professors in a number of ways. One of the biggest effects is in the replacement of tenure-track faculty positions with part-time instructors. These part-time instructors include adjunct faculty, visiting professors, and graduate students. Organizations such as the American Association of University Professors and the American Federation of Teachers are working to prevent the loss of these full-time jobs, as well as to help part-time instructors receive better pay and benefits. Other issues involve the development of long-distance education departments in many schools. Though these correspondence courses have become very popular in recent years, many professionals believe that students in long-distance education programs receive only a second-rate education. A related concern is about the proliferation of computers in the classroom. Some courses consist only of instruction by computer software and the Internet. The effects of these alternative methods on the teaching profession will be offset somewhat by the expected increases in college enrollment in coming years.

FOR MORE INFORMATION

To read about the issues affecting college professors, contact the following organizations:

American Association of University Professors
1012 14th Street, NW, Suite 500
Washington, DC 20005-3406
Tel: 202-737-5900
Email: aaup@aaup.org
http://www.aaup.org

American Federation of Teachers
555 New Jersey Avenue, NW
Washington, DC 20001-2029
Tel: 202-879-4400
Email: online@aft.org
http://www.aft.org

Environmental Technicians

OVERVIEW

Environmental technicians, also known as *pollution control technicians*, conduct tests and field investigations to obtain soil samples and other data. Their research is used by engineers, scientists, and others who help clean up, monitor, control, or prevent pollution. An environmental technician usually specializes in air, water, or soil pollution. Although work differs by employer and specialty, technicians generally collect samples for laboratory analysis with specialized instruments and equipment; monitor pollution control devices and systems, such as smokestack air "scrubbers"; and perform various other tests and investigations to evaluate pollution problems. They follow strict procedures in collecting and recording data in order to meet the requirements of environmental laws.

In general, environmental technicians do not operate the equipment and systems designed to prevent pollution or remove pollutants. Instead, they test environmental conditions. In addition, some analyze and report on their findings. There are approximately 31,000 environmental science and protection technicians, including health technicians, in the United States.

QUICK FACTS

School Subjects
Biology
Chemistry

Personal Skills
Mechanical/manipulative
Technical/scientific

Work Environment
Indoors and outdoors
One location with some
   travel

Minimum Education Level
Some postsecondary training

Salary Range
$23,600 to $38,090 to
   $70,000+

Certification or Licensing
Required for certain positions

Outlook
About as fast as the average

DOT
029

GOE
02.05.02

NOC
2231

O*NET-SOC
19-2041.00, 19-4091.00

HISTORY

Stricter pollution control regulations of the mid-1960s to early 1970s created a job market for environmental technicians. As regulations on industry have become more stringent, the job has grown both in importance and in scope. For centuries, the biosphere (the self-regulating "envelope" of air, water, and land in which all life on earth exists) was generally able to scatter, break down, or adapt to all the wastes and pollution produced by people.

This began to change drastically with the industrial revolution. Beginning in England in the 1750s, the industrial revolution caused the shift from a farming society to an industrialized society. Although it had many economic benefits, industrialization took a terrible toll on the environment. Textile manufacturing and iron processing spread through England, and coal-powered mills, machines, and factories spewed heavy black smoke into the air. Rivers and lakes became open sewers as factories dumped their wastes. By the 19th century, areas with high population density and clusters of factories were experiencing markedly higher death and disease rates than areas with little industrial development.

The industrial revolution spread all over the world, including France in the 1830s; Germany in the 1850s; the United States after the Civil War; and Russia and Asia (especially Japan) at the turn of the century. Wherever industry took hold, there were warning signs that the biosphere could not handle the resulting pollution. Smoke and smog hung over large cities from their many factories. Residents experienced more respiratory and other health problems. Manufacturing wastes and untreated sewage poisoned surface waters and underground sources of water, affecting water supplies and increasing disease. Wastes and pollution also seeped into the soil, affecting crops.

After World War II, the development of new synthetic materials and their resulting waste products, including plastics, pesticides, and vehicle exhaust that are difficult to degrade (break down) worsened pollution problems. Fish and wildlife began to die because rivers and lakes were choked with chemicals and wastes. Scientists documented connections between pollution and birth defects, cancer, fertility problems, genetic damage, and many other serious problems.

Not until the mid-1960s to early 1970s did public outcry, environmental activism, and political and economic necessity force the passage of stricter pollution control laws. Federal environmental legislation mandated cleanups of existing air, water, and soil pollution, and began to limit the type and amount of polluting substances that industry could release into the environment. Manufacturers were required to operate within stricter guidelines for air emissions, wastewater treatment and disposal, and other polluting activities. States and municipalities also were given increasing responsibilities for monitoring and working to reduce levels of auto, industrial, and other pollution. Out of the need to meet these new requirements,

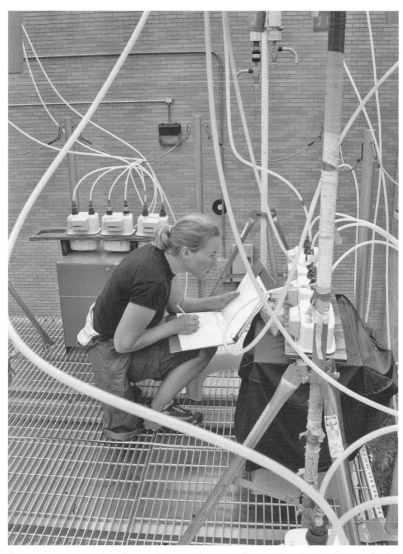

An environmental technician records air pollution levels on the roof of a building with a mobile air pollution lab. *(Jim West, The Image Works)*

the pollution control industry was born—and with it, the job of environmental technician.

THE JOB

Environmental technicians usually specialize in one aspect of pollution control, such as water pollution, air pollution, or soil pollution.

Sampling, monitoring, and testing are the major activities of the job. No matter what their specialty, environmental technicians work largely for or with government agencies that regulate pollution by industry. The following paragraphs describe specialties in the field.

Water pollution technicians monitor both industrial and residential discharge, such as from wastewater treatment plants. They help to determine the presence and extent of pollutants in water. They collect samples from lakes, streams, rivers, groundwater (the water under the earth), industrial or municipal wastewater, or other sources. Samples are brought to labs, where chemical and other tests are performed. If the samples contain harmful substances, remedial (cleanup) actions will need to be taken. These technicians also may perform various field tests, such as checking the pH, oxygen, and nitrate level of surface waters.

Some water pollution technicians set up monitoring equipment to obtain information on water flow, movement, temperature, or pressure and record readings from these devices. To trace flow patterns, they may inject dyes into the water.

Technicians have to be careful not to contaminate their samples, stray from the specific testing procedure, or otherwise do something to ruin the sample or cause faulty or misleading results.

Depending on the specific job, water pollution technicians may spend a good part of their time outdoors, in good weather and bad, aboard boats, and sometimes near unpleasant smells or potentially hazardous substances. Field sites may be in remote areas. In some cases, the technician may have to fly to a different part of the country, perhaps staying away from home for a long period.

Water pollution technicians play a big role in industrial wastewater discharge monitoring, treatment, and control. Nearly every manufacturing process produces wastewater, but U.S. manufacturers today are required to be more careful about what they discharge with their wastewater.

Some water pollution technicians specialize in groundwater, ocean water, or other types of natural waters. *Estuarine resource technicians,* for example, specialize in estuary waters, or coastal areas where fresh water and salt water come together. These bays, salt marshes, inlets, and other tidal water bodies support a wide variety of plant and animal life with ecologically complex relationships. They are vulnerable to destructive pollution from adjoining industries, cities and towns, and other sources. Estuarine resource technicians aid scientists in studying the resulting environmental changes. They may work in laboratories or aboard boats, or may use diving gear to collect samples directly.

Air pollution technicians collect and test air samples (for example, from chimneys of industrial manufacturing plants), record data on atmospheric conditions (such as determining levels of airborne substances from auto or industrial emissions), and supply data to scientists and engineers for further testing and analysis. In labs, air pollution technicians may help test air samples or re-create contaminants. They may use atomic absorption spectrophotometers, flame photometers, gas chromatographs, and other instruments for analyzing samples.

In the field, air pollution technicians may use rooftop sampling devices or operate mobile monitoring units or stationary trailers. The trailers may be equipped with elaborate automatic testing systems, including some of the same devices found in laboratories. Outside air is pumped into various chambers in the trailer where it is analyzed for the presence of pollutants. The results can be recorded by machine on 30-day rolls of graph paper or fed into a computer at regular intervals. Technicians set up and maintain the sampling devices, replenish the chemicals used in tests, replace worn parts, calibrate instruments, and record results. Some air pollution technicians specialize in certain pollutants or pollution sources. For example, *engine emission technicians* focus on exhaust from internal combustion engines.

Soil or *land pollution technicians* collect soil, silt, or mud samples and check them for contamination. Soil can become contaminated when polluted water seeps into the earth, such as when liquid waste leaks from a landfill or other source into surrounding ground. Soil pollution technicians work for federal, state, and local government agencies, for private consulting firms, and elsewhere. (Some soil conservation technicians perform pollution control work.)

A position sometimes grouped with other environmental technicians is that of *noise pollution technician*. Noise pollution technicians use rooftop devices and mobile units to take readings and collect data on noise levels of factories, highways, airports, and other locations in order to determine noise exposure levels for workers or the public. Some test noise levels of construction equipment, chain saws, snow blowers, lawn mowers, or other equipment.

REQUIREMENTS

High School
In high school, key courses include biology, chemistry, and physics. Conservation or ecology courses also will be useful, if offered at your school. Math classes should include at least algebra and

geometry, and taking English and speech classes will help to sharpen your communications skills. In addition, work on developing your computer skills while in high school, either on your own or through a class.

Postsecondary Training

Some technician positions call for a high school diploma plus employer training. As environmental work becomes more technical and complex, more positions are being filled by technicians with at least an associate's degree. To meet this need, many community colleges across the country have developed appropriate programs for environmental technicians. Areas of study include environmental engineering technologies, pollution control technologies, conservation, and ecology. Courses include meteorology, toxicology, source testing, sampling, and analysis, air quality management, environmental science, and statistics. Other training requirements vary by employer. Some experts advise attending school in the part of the country where you'd like to begin your career so you can start getting to know local employers before you graduate.

Certification or Licensing

Certification or licensing is required for some positions in pollution control, especially those in which sanitation, public health, a public water supply, or a sewage treatment system is involved. For example, the Institute of Professional Environmental Practice offers the qualified environmental professional and the environmental professional intern certifications. See the end of this article for contact information.

Other Requirements

Environmental technicians should be curious, patient, detail-oriented, and capable of following instructions. Basic manual skills are essential for collecting samples and performing similar tasks. Complex environmental regulations drive technicians' jobs; therefore, it's crucial that they are able to read and understand technical materials and to carefully follow any written guidelines for sampling or other procedures. Computer skills and the ability to read and interpret maps, charts, and diagrams are also necessary.

Technicians must make accurate and objective observations, maintain clear and complete records, and be exact in their computations. In addition, good physical conditioning is a requirement for some activities, for example, climbing up smokestacks to take emission samples.

EXPLORING

To learn more about environmental jobs, visit your local library and read some technical and general-interest publications in environmental science. This might give you an idea of the technologies being used and issues being discussed in the field today. You also can visit a municipal health department or pollution control agency in your community. Many agencies are pleased to explain their work to visitors.

School science clubs, local community groups, and naturalist clubs can help broaden your understanding of various aspects of the natural world and give you some experience. Most schools have recycling programs that enlist student help.

With the help of a teacher or career counselor, a tour of a local manufacturing plant using an air- or water-pollution abatement system also might be arranged. Many plants offer tours of their operations to the public. This should provide an excellent opportunity to see technicians at work.

As a high school student, it may be difficult to obtain summer or part-time work as a technician due to the extensive operations and safety training required for some of these jobs. However, it is worthwhile to check with a local environmental agency, nonprofit environmental organizations, or private consulting firms to learn of volunteer or paid support opportunities. Any hands-on experience you can get will be of value to a future employer.

EMPLOYERS

Approximately 31,000 environmental science and protection technicians are employed in the United States. Many environmental technicians work for government agencies that monitor the environment, such as the Environmental Protection Agency (EPA), and the Departments of Agriculture, Energy, and Interior.

Water pollution technicians may be employed by manufacturers that produce wastewater, municipal wastewater treatment facilities, private firms hired to monitor or control pollutants in water or wastewater, and government regulatory agencies responsible for protecting water quality.

Air pollution technicians work for government agencies such as regional EPA offices. They also work for private manufacturers producing airborne pollutants, research facilities, pollution control equipment manufacturers, and other employers.

Soil pollution technicians may work for federal or state departments of agriculture and EPA offices. They also work for private agricultural groups that monitor soil quality for pesticide levels.

Noise pollution technicians are employed by private companies and by government agencies such as the Occupational Safety and Health Administration.

STARTING OUT

Graduates of two-year environmental programs are often employed during their final term by recruiters who visit their schools. Specific opportunities will vary depending on the part of the country, the segment of the environmental industry, the specialization of the technician (air, water, or land), the economy, and other factors. Many beginning technicians find the greatest number of positions available in state or local government agencies.

Most schools provide job-hunting advice and assistance. Direct application to state or local environmental agencies, employment agencies, or potential employers can also be a productive approach. If you hope to find employment outside your current geographic area, you may get good results by checking with professional organizations or by reading advertisements in technical journals, many of which have searchable job listings on the Internet.

ADVANCEMENT

The typical hierarchy for environmental work is technician (two years of postsecondary education or less), technologist (two years or more of postsecondary training), technician manager (perhaps a technician or technologist with many years of experience), and scientist or engineer (four-year bachelor of science degree or more, up to Ph.D. level).

In some private manufacturing or consulting firms, technician positions are used for training newly recruited professional staff. In such cases, workers with four-year degrees in engineering or physical science are likely to be promoted before those with two-year degrees. Employees of government agencies usually are organized under civil service systems that specify experience, education, and other criteria for advancement. Private industry promotions are structured differently and will depend on a variety of factors.

EARNINGS

Pay for environmental technicians varies widely depending on the nature of the work they do, training and experience required for the work, type of employer, geographic region, and other factors. Public-sector positions tend to pay less than private-sector positions.

Earnings of energy conservation technicians vary significantly based on their amount of formal training and experience. According to the U.S. Department of Labor, the average annual salary for environmental science and protection technicians was $38,090 in 2006. Salaries ranged from less than $23,600 to more than $60,700. Technicians who worked for local government earned mean annual salaries of $43,050 in 2006; those who were employed by state government earned $43,810. Technicians who become managers or supervisors can earn up to $70,000 per year or more. Technicians who work in private industry or who further their education to secure teaching positions can also expect to earn higher than average salaries.

No matter which area they specialize in, environmental technicians generally enjoy fringe benefits such as paid vacation, holidays and sick time, and employer-paid training. Technicians who work full time (and some who work part time) often have health insurance benefits. Technicians employed by the federal government may get additional benefits such as pension and retirement benefits.

WORK ENVIRONMENT

Conditions range from clean and pleasant indoor offices and laboratories to hot, cold, wet, bad-smelling, noisy, or even hazardous settings outdoors. Anyone planning a career in environmental technology should realize the possibility of exposure to unpleasant or unsafe conditions at least occasionally in his or her career. Employers often can minimize these negatives through special equipment and procedures. Most laboratories and manufacturing companies have safety procedures for potentially dangerous situations.

Some jobs involve vigorous physical activity, such as handling a small boat or climbing a tall ladder. For the most part, technicians need only to be prepared for moderate activity. Travel may be required; technicians travel to urban, industrial, or rural settings for sampling.

Because their job can involve a considerable amount of repetitive work, patience and the ability to handle routine are important. Yet, particularly when environmental technicians are working in the field, they also have to be ready to use their resourcefulness and ingenuity to find the best ways of responding to new situations.

OUTLOOK

Demand for environmental technicians is expected to increase about as fast as the average for all occupations through 2014. Those trained to handle increasingly complex technical demands will have the best employment prospects. Environmental technicians will be needed to regulate waste products; to collect air, water, and soil samples for measuring levels of pollutants; to monitor compliance with environmental regulations; and to clean up contaminated sites.

Demand will be higher in some areas of the country than others depending on specialty; for example, air pollution technicians will be especially in demand in large cities, such as Los Angeles and New York, which face pressure to comply with national air quality standards. Amount of industrialization, stringency of state and local pollution control enforcement, health of local economy, and other factors also will affect demand by region and specialty. Perhaps the greatest factors affecting environmental work are continued mandates for pollution control by the federal government. As long as the federal government is supporting pollution control, the environmental technician will be needed.

FOR MORE INFORMATION

For job listings and certification information, contact
Air & Waste Management Association
420 Fort Duquesne Boulevard
One Gateway Center, Third Floor
Pittsburgh, PA 15222-1435
Tel: 412-232-3444
Email: info@awma.org
http://www.awma.org

For information on the engineering field and technician certification, contact
American Society of Certified Engineering Technicians
PO Box 1536
Brandon, MS 39043-1536
Tel: 601-824-8991
http://www.ascet.org

The following organization is an environmental careers resource for high school and college students.
Environmental Careers Organization
30 Winter Street
Boston, MA 02108-4720
Tel: 617-426-4783
http://www.eco.org

For information on environmental careers and student employment opportunities, contact
Environmental Protection Agency
Ariel Rios Building
1200 Pennsylvania Avenue, NW
Washington, DC 20460-0001
Tel: 202-260-2090
Email: public-access@epa.gov
http://www.epa.gov

For information on certification, contact
Institute of Professional Environmental Practice
600 Forbes Avenue
333 Fisher Hall
Pittsburgh, PA 15282-0001
Email: ipep@duq.edu
http://www.ipep.org

For job listings and scholarship opportunities, contact
National Ground Water Association
601 Dempsey Road
Westerville, OH 43081-8978
Tel: 800-551-7379
Email: ngwa@ngwa.org
http://www.ngwa.org

For information on conferences and workshops, contact
Water Environment Federation
601 Wythe Street
Alexandria, VA 22314-1994
Tel: 800-666-0206
http://www.wef.org

Food Technologists

QUICK FACTS

School Subjects
Chemistry
Mathematics

Personal Skills
Following instructions
Technical/scientific

Work Environment
Primarily indoors
Primarily one location

Minimum Education Level
Bachelor's degree

Salary Range
$29,620 to $73,150 to
$97,350+

Certification or Licensing
Voluntary

Outlook
About as fast as the average

DOT
041

GOE
02.03.04

NOC
N/A

O*NET-SOC
19-1012.00, 19-4011.02

OVERVIEW

Food technologists, sometimes known as *food scientists,* study the physical, chemical, and biological composition of food. They develop methods for safely processing, preserving, and packaging food and search for ways to improve its flavor and nutritional value. They also conduct tests to ensure that products, from fresh produce to packaged meals, meet industry and government standards. Approximately 8,700 food technologists are employed in the United States.

HISTORY

One of the earliest methods of food preservation was drying. Grains were sun- and air-dried to prevent mold growth and insect damage. Fruits and vegetables dried in the sun and meats dried and smoked over a fire were stored for use during times of need. Fruits were preserved by fermenting them into wines and vinegars, and fermented milk became curds, cheeses, and yogurts.

Methods of food preservation improved over the centuries, but there were severe limitations until the evolution of scientific methods made it possible to preserve food. By creating conditions unfavorable to the growth or survival of spoilage microorganisms and preventing deterioration by enzymes, scientists were able to extend the storage life of foods well beyond the normal period.

For most of history, people bought or traded for bulk foods, such as grain or rice, rather than prepared foods. This began to change in the early 1800s, when new methods of preserving and packaging foods were developed. The science of food technology did not, however, really develop until shortly before the American entrance into World War II. Prompted by the need to supply U.S. troops with nutritious, flavorful foods that were not only easy to transport but also kept for long periods of time, scientists around 1940 began making great advances in the preparation, preservation, and packaging of foods. By the 1950s, food science and food technology departments were being established by many universities, and food science disciplines became important and respected areas of study.

Another boost to the food technology program came with the U.S. space program; new types of foods, as well as new types of preparation, packaging, and processing were needed to feed astronauts in space.

By the late 20th century, few people still canned or preserved their own fruits and vegetables. Advances in production methods in this century have made it possible to process larger quantities of a wider range of food products. Scientists specializing in food technology have found better ways to retard spoilage, improve flavor, and provide foods that are consistent in quality, flavor, texture, and size. Innovations such as freeze drying, irradiation, and artificial coloring and flavoring have changed the way many of the foods we eat are processed and prepared. Consumer demand for an ever-increasing variety of foods has created a demand for food technologists to develop them. Foods processed in a variety of ways are readily available to the consumer and have become such an accepted part of modern life that one rarely gives a thought to the complexities involved. The safety of the process, nutrition, development of new products and production methods, and the packaging of products are all the responsibility of food technologists.

THE JOB

Food technologists usually specialize in one phase of food technology. About one-third are involved in research and development. A large number are employed in quality-control laboratories or in the production or processing areas of food plants. Others teach or perform basic research in colleges and universities, work in sales or management positions, or are employed as technical writers or consultants. The branches of food technology are numerous and include cereal grains, meat and poultry, fats and oils, seafood, animal foods, beverages, dairy products, flavors, sugar and starches, stabilizers, preservatives, colors, and nutritional additives.

Food technologists in basic research study the structure and composition of food and observe the changes that take place during storage or processing. The knowledge they gain may enable them to develop new sources of proteins, determine the effects of processing on microorganisms, or isolate factors that affect the flavor, appearance, or texture of foods. Technologists engaged in applied research and development have the more practical task of creating new food products and developing new processing methods. They also continue to work with existing foods to make them more nutritious and flavorful and to improve their color and texture.

A rapidly growing area of food technology is biotechnology. Food technologists in this area work with plant breeding, gene splicing, microbial fermentation, and plant cell tissue cultures to produce enhanced raw products for processing.

Foods may lose their characteristics and nutritious value during processing and storage. Food technologists seek ways to prevent this by developing improved methods for processing, production, quality control, packaging, and distribution. They conduct chemical and microbiological tests on products to be sure they conform to standards set by the government and by the food industry. They also determine the nutritive content (the amounts of sugar, starch, protein, fat, vitamins, and minerals) that federal regulations say must be printed on the labels.

Food technologists in quality-control laboratories concentrate on ensuring that foods in every stage of processing meet industry and government standards. They check to see that raw ingredients are fresh, sufficiently ripe, and suitable for processing. They conduct periodic inspections of processing line operations. They also test after processing to be sure that various enzymes are not active and that bacteria levels are low enough so the food will not spoil or be unsafe to eat.

Some technologists test new products in test kitchens or develop new processing methods in laboratory pilot plants. Others devise new methods for packaging and storing foods. To solve problems, they may confer with processing engineers, flavor experts, or packaging and marketing specialists.

In processing plants, food technologists are responsible for preparing production specifications and scheduling processing operations. They ensure that proper temperature and humidity levels are maintained in storage areas and that wastes are disposed of properly and other sanitary regulations are observed throughout the plant. They also make recommendations to management in matters relating to efficiency or economy, such as new equipment or suppliers.

Some food technologists have positions in other fields where they can apply their specialized knowledge to such areas as advertising, market research, or technical sales.

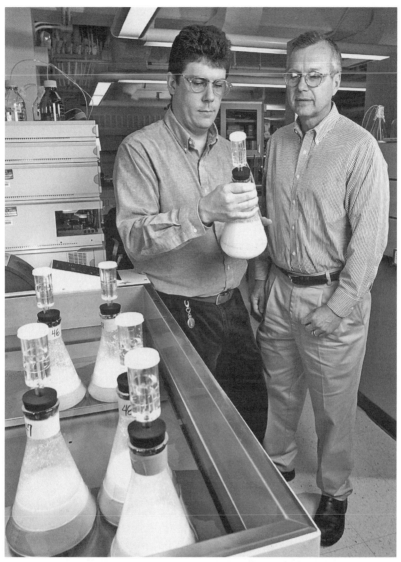

A food technologist (left) and researcher check fermentability of enzymatically milled corn. *(Stephen Ausmus, Agricultural Research Service, U.S. Department of Agriculture)*

REQUIREMENTS

High School

You can prepare for a career in food technology by taking plenty of high school science courses. Be sure to take biology, chemistry, and physics. To get hands-on experience working with food, take family and consumer science classes. Four years of mathematics classes, English classes, computer science classes, and other college-preparatory courses are also important to take.

Postsecondary Training
Educational requirements for this field are high. Beginners need at least a bachelor's degree in food technology, food science, or food engineering. Some technologists hold degrees in other areas, such as chemistry, biology, engineering, agriculture, or business, and nearly half have advanced degrees. Master's degrees and doctorates are mandatory for college teaching and are usually necessary for management and research positions.

More than 45 schools in the United States, Canada, and Mexico offer the course work needed to become a food technologist, and many of these programs have been approved by the Institute of Food Technologists. See the institute's Web site (http://www.ift.org) for approved school information. Typical courses include physics, biochemistry, mathematics, microbiology, the social sciences and humanities, and business administration as well as food technology courses including food preservation, processing, sanitation, and marketing. Most of these schools also offer advanced degrees, usually in specialized areas of food technology. To successfully complete their program, candidates for a master's degree or a doctoral degree must perform extensive research and write a thesis reporting their original findings. Specialists in administrative, managerial, or regulatory areas may earn advanced degrees in business administration or in law rather than in food technology.

Other Requirements
Food technologists should have analytical minds and enjoy technical work. In addition, they must be able to express themselves clearly and be detail oriented. They also must be able to work well in group situations and participate and contribute to a team effort.

EXPLORING
Students may be able to arrange field trips to local food processing plants and plan interviews with or lectures by experts in the field. Apart from an interest in science, and especially chemistry, prospective food technologists may also develop interests in cooking and in inventing their own recipes.

Typical Undergraduate Courses in Food Science

- Biochemistry
- Biology
- Calculus
- Food Analysis
- Food Chemistry
- Food Engineering
- Food Laws and Regulatory Processes
- Food Microbiology
- Food Processing
- Food Quality Assurance
- General Chemistry
- General Physics
- Mathematics
- Nutrition
- Organic Chemistry
- Physical Chemistry
- Statistics

Because of the educational requirements for food technologists, it is not likely that students will be able to acquire actual experience while still in high school. Part-time and summer employment as workers in food processing plants, however, would provide an excellent overview of the industry. More advanced college students may have opportunities for jobs helping out in research laboratories.

EMPLOYERS

There are approximately 8,700 food technologists employed in the United States. Food technologists work in a wide variety of settings, including food processing plants, food ingredient plants, and food manufacturing plants. They may work in basic research, product development, processing and quality assurance, packaging, or market research. There are positions in laboratories, test kitchens, and on production lines as well as with government agencies.

STARTING OUT

Many schools offering degree programs in food science will also offer job placement assistance. Also, recruiters from private industry frequently conduct interviews on campus. Faculty members may be willing to grant referrals to exceptional students. Another method is to make direct application to individual companies.

Frequently, the food products with which food technologists work determine where they are employed. Those who work with meats or grains may work in the Midwest. Technologists who work with citrus fruits usually work in Florida or California. Two-thirds of all food technologists are employed by private industry and the rest work for the federal government. Some major government employers of food technologists include the Environmental Protection Agency, National Aeronautics and Space Administration, the Food and Drug Administration, and the United States Department of Agriculture.

ADVANCEMENT

For food technologists with a bachelor's degree, there are two general paths to advancement, depending on whether they work in production or in research. They may begin as quality-assurance chemists or assistant production managers and, with experience, move up to more responsible management positions. Some technologists may start as junior food chemists in the research and development laboratory of a food company and advance to section head or another research management position.

Technologists who hold master's degrees may start out as food chemists in a research and development laboratory. Those with doctorates usually begin their careers in basic research or teaching. Other food technologists may gain expertise in more specialized areas and become sensory evaluation experts or food-marketing specialists.

EARNINGS

According to the U.S. Department of Labor, median annual earnings of food scientists and technologists were $53,810 in 2006. The highest paid workers earned more than $97,350, and the lowest paid earned less than $29,620.

The Institute of Food Technologists reports that its members earned a median salary of $73,150 in 2003. IFT members with a bachelor's degree in food science earned a median salary of $65,000. Members with a master's degree earned a median of $73,500, those with a Ph.D. earned a median of $85,000, and those with an M.B.A. degree earned a median of $95,000 a year.

Most food technologists will receive generous benefit plans, which usually include health insurance, life insurance, pension plans, and vacation and sick pay. Others may receive funds for continuing education.

WORK ENVIRONMENT

Most food technologists work regular hours in clean, well-lighted, temperature-controlled offices, laboratories, or classrooms. Technologists in production and quality control who work in processing plants may be subject to machine noise and hot or cold conditions.

OUTLOOK

The food industry is the largest single industry in the United States and throughout the world. Because people have to eat, there will always be a need for people to develop, test, and process food products. In developed countries, the ever-present consumer demand for new and different food products means that food scientists and technologists will always be in demand.

Several factors have also created continuing demand for skilled technologists. New labeling laws enacted in the 1990s have required companies to provide detailed nutritional information on their products. The continuing trend toward more healthful eating habits has recently focused on the roles of fats, cholesterol, and salt in nutrition, and companies have rushed to create a variety of low-fat, low-sodium, fat-free, cholesterol-free, and sodium-free foods. A larger and more varied supply of wholesome and economical food is needed to satisfy current tastes. The food industry will have to produce convenience foods of greater quality for use in homes and for the food service institutions that supply airlines, restaurants, and other major customers. More technologists may be hired to research and produce new foods from modifications of wheat, corn, rice, and soybeans, such as the "meat" products made from vegetable proteins. The food industry has increased its spending in recent years for this kind of research and development and is likely to continue to do so. Developing these products, without sacrificing such important factors as taste, appearance, and texture, has produced many new opportunities for food technologists. Food technologists will also be sought to produce new foods for poor and starving people in underdeveloped countries. Experienced technologists will use their advanced training to create new foods from such staples as rice, corn, wheat, and soybeans.

An increasing focus on food safety and biosecurity will also create demand for food technologists with knowledge of these practice areas.

Finally, the increasing emphasis on the automation of many elements of food processing has also created a need for food technologists to adapt cooking and preparation processes to the new technology.

FOR MORE INFORMATION

For consumer fact sheets, information on issues in the food science industry, and food safety news, visit the association's Web site or contact
Grocery Manufacturers/Food Products Association
1350 I Street, NW, Suite 300
Washington, DC 20005-3377
Tel: 202-639-5900
http://www.fpa-food.org

For information on accredited food science programs and to order the booklet Finding Your First Job in Food Science, *visit the IFT's Web site.*
Institute of Food Technologists (IFT)
525 West Van Buren, Suite 1000
Chicago, IL 60607-3830
Tel: 800-438-3663
Email: info@ift.org
http://www.ift.org

For national news on agriculture and food issues, contact
U.S. Department of Agriculture
1400 Independence Avenue, SW
Washington, DC 20250-0002
http://www.usda.gov

For comprehensive information on careers, educational programs, and scholarships, visit
Careers in Food Science
http://school.discovery.com/foodscience/college_resources.html

———— INTERVIEW ————

Dr. Faye Dong, professor and head of the Department of Food Science and Human Nutrition at the University of Illinois at Urbana–Champaign, discussed food science with the editors of Careers in Focus: Chemistry.

Q. Please tell us about your program.
A. Our Department of Food Science and Human Nutrition (FSHN) offers bachelor's of science (B.S.), master's of science (M.S.),

and Ph.D. degrees in food science. We have approximately 50 students in our Institute of Food Technologists–approved B.S. degree program, and approximately 50 graduate students studying for M.S. or Ph.D. degrees. Visit http://www.fshn.uiuc. edu to learn more about the program.

Q. Can you tell us about the internship opportunities that are available to students at your school?

A. FSHN has close working relationships with many food companies located in the greater Chicago area, as well as with companies located nationally and internationally.

During the school year, our undergraduate and graduate students have the opportunity to attend many information sessions with recruiters who come to our department to give presentations about their companies. In the same visit, these recruiters interview our students for internships and for entry-level positions in the company. We strongly encourage our undergraduate students to apply for summer internships, particularly after their sophomore and junior years because the experience, knowledge, and professional and interpersonal skills that the students acquire are a very valuable part of their education and preparation for future careers. Some graduate students, with the permission of their major professors, have the opportunity to participate in internships at food companies. At the end of the internship experience, some students receive job offers from the food company.

Q. What is one thing that young people may not know about a career in food science?

A. A career in food science can be in the food industry, in government agencies, and in academia.

The **food industry** is very exciting, fast paced, and presents an opportunity to contribute to the nutritional, convenience, safety, and environmental aspects of food products. Food science is about food and it is a science-based discipline, so employees in the food industry need to keep up with current research and regulations related to food.

Government agencies, such as the U.S. Food and Drug Administration and the U.S. Department of Agriculture, play important roles in ensuring the safety of our food supply. Positions can be focused on regulation/compliance or on research.

Universities also hire food scientists. As tenure-track faculty members (Ph.D. degree), food scientists engage in teaching, research, and outreach activities. As lecturers (M.S. or Ph.D.

degrees), they will be involved in teaching and outreach activities. As lab technicians (B.S. or M.S. degrees), food scientists will be focused on research.

Q. What types of students pursue food science study in your program?

A. Students in our food science program are interested in food from the perspectives of food science, food technology, health aspects, and culinary applications. They enjoy the science, such as the chemistry and microbiology, and learning how principles in those disciplines apply to food systems.

Q. What advice would you offer food science majors as they graduate and look for jobs?

A. Most students pursue positions in the food industry. We advise that, while they are here in school, they should take the opportunity to develop their knowledge base, critical thinking skills, and ability to solve problems. We also encourage them to develop their professional and interpersonal skills: be familiar with computer programs; be adept at using basic laboratory and pilot plant equipment; and interpersonally, to know how to get along with others, work well on teams, develop leadership skills, write and speak well, behave professionally, and to have high ethical standards. Learning and practicing these skills are a part of our curriculum. We also emphasize that they should continue to learn for the rest of their careers.

Q. Are there any changes in this job market that students should expect?

A. It has become increasingly important for students to have an understanding of the different fields associated with the food industry. They should understand basic concepts of business, marketing, economics, food laws and regulations, and consumer trends. There is usually a steep learning curve during the first couple of years in a new job when entry-level employees pick up some of this information. Also, many students after they graduate will pursue a business degree in the evening while they are employed.

Students should not expect to be working with a single food commodity. In contrast to the past, today's manufactured foods are usually a combination of several commodities—take pizza, for example! Students should also be nimble and be ready to experience company buyouts and mergers. They should expect that during their career, chances are that they will change jobs more than once.

Forensic Experts

OVERVIEW

Forensic experts apply scientific principles and methods to the analysis, identification, and classification of physical evidence relating to criminal (or suspected criminal) cases. They do much of their work in laboratories, where they subject evidence to tests and then record the results. They may travel to crime scenes to collect evidence and record the physical facts of a site. Forensic experts may also be called upon to testify as expert witnesses and to present scientific findings in court.

HISTORY

In Scotland during the late 1780s, a man was convicted of murder when the soles of his boots matched a plaster cast of footprints taken from the scene of the crime. This is one of the earliest recorded cases of the use of physical evidence to link a suspected criminal with the crime.

In the late 19th century, scientists learned to analyze and classify poisons so their presence could be traced in a body. At about the same time, a controversy arose over the different methods being used to identify individuals positively. Fingerprinting emerged in the early 20th century as the most reliable method of personal identification. With the advent of X-ray technology, experts could rely on dental records to substitute for fingerprint analysis when a corpse was in advanced stages of decomposition and the condition of the skin had deteriorated.

Forensic pathology (medical examination of suspicious or unexplained deaths) also came into prominence at this time, as did ballistics, which is the study of projectiles and how they are shot from firearms.

QUICK FACTS

School Subjects
Biology
Chemistry

Personal Skills
Following instructions
Technical/scientific

Work Environment
Primarily indoors
Primarily multiple locations

Minimum Education Level
Bachelor's degree

Salary Range
$20,000 to $45,330 to $100,000+

Certification or Licensing
None available

Outlook
Much faster than the average

DOT
188

GOE
04.03.02

NOC
N/A

O*NET-SOC
19-4092.00

The study of ballistics was aided by the invention of the comparison microscope, which enabled an investigator to look at bullets side by side and compare their individual markings. Since individual gun barrels "scar" bullets in a unique pattern, similar markings found on different bullets may prove that they were fired from the same weapon.

These investigations by pioneer forensic scientists led the courts and the police to acknowledge the value of scientifically examined physical evidence in establishing guilt or innocence, confirming identity, proving authenticity of documents, and establishing cause of death. As the result of this acceptance by the legal and law enforcement communities, crime laboratories were established. One of the first, largest, and most complete laboratories is that of the Federal Bureau of Investigation (FBI), founded in 1932. Today, the FBI laboratory examines many thousands of pieces of evidence each year, and its employees present their findings in trials all over the United States and around the world. As the forensic sciences proved their worth, crime laboratories were established in larger cities and by state police departments. These laboratories are used in turn by many communities too small to support labs of their own. The scientific analysis of evidence has become an accepted part of police procedure, and new forensic advances, such as DNA testing, are being developed every day.

THE JOB

Forensic experts, also called *criminalists,* use the instruments of science and engineering to examine physical evidence. They use spectroscopes, microscopes, gas chromatographs, infrared and ultraviolet light, microphotography, and other lab measuring and testing equipment to analyze fibers, fabric, dust, soils, paint chips, glass fragments, fire accelerants, paper and ink, and other substances in order to identify their composition and origin. They analyze poisons, drugs, and other substances found in bodies by examining tissue samples, stomach contents, and blood samples. They analyze and classify blood, blood alcohol, semen, hair, fingernails, teeth, human and animal bones and tissue, and other biological specimens. Using samples of the DNA in these materials, they can match a person with a sample of body tissue. They study documents to determine whether they are forged or genuine. They also examine the physical properties of firearms, bullets, and explosives.

At the scene of a crime (whether actual or suspected), forensic experts collect and label evidence. This painstaking task may involve searching for spent bullets or bits of an exploded bomb and other objects scattered by an explosion. They might look for footprints, fingerprints, and tire tracks, which must be recorded or preserved by plaster casting before they are wiped out. Since crime scenes must eventually be cleaned up, forensic experts take notes and photographs to preserve the arrangement of objects, bodies, and debris. They are sometimes called on later to reconstruct the scene of a crime by making a floor plan or map pinpointing the exact location of bodies, weapons, and furniture.

One important discipline within forensic science is identification. *Fingerprint classifiers* catalog and compare fingerprints of suspected criminals with records to determine if the people who left the fingerprints at the scene of a crime were involved in previous crimes. They often try to match the fingerprints of unknown corpses with fingerprint records to establish their identities. They work in laboratories and offices, and travel to other areas such as crime scenes. Retrieving fingerprints outside may be difficult and require specialized processes, such as dusting glassware, windows, or walls with a fine powder. This powder contrasts with many different surfaces and will highlight any fingerprints that remain. Another method of retrieving fingerprints is to lift them off with a flexible tape, which can be brought back to the laboratory for further evaluation and matching.

Fingerprint classifiers compare new prints against those found after the commission of similar crimes. The classifier documents this information and transfers it to the main record-keeping system, often a large mainframe computer system. In the last decade or so, computers have greatly enhanced the possibility of matching new fingerprints to those already on file. A fingerprint classifier may keep individual files on current crimes and note any similarities between them.

Identification technicians work at various jobs related to maintaining police records. In addition to handling fingerprint records, they also work with other kinds of records, such as police reports and eyewitness information about crimes and accidents. They operate equipment used to microfilm police records, as well as store the microfilm and retrieve or copy records upon the request of police or other public officials. *Forensic pathologists* perform autopsies to determine the cause of death; autopsies are almost always performed on victims of crime. *Forensic psychiatrists* also conduct psychiatric evaluations of accused criminals and are often called to testify on whether the accused is mentally fit to stand trial.

Molecular biologists and *geneticists* analyze and review forensic and paternity samples, provide expert testimony in civil and criminal trials, and identify and develop new technologies for use in human identification.

Other job titles within forensic science include *forensic toxicologists,* who are concerned with detecting and identifying the presence of poisons or drugs in a victim's body; *forensic odontologists,* who use dental records and evidence to identify crime victims and to investigate bite marks; and *forensic anthropologists,* who examine and identify bones and skeletal remains.

Forensic experts spend the bulk of their time in the laboratory working with physical evidence. They seldom have direct contact with persons involved in actual or suspected crimes or with police investigators except when collecting evidence and reporting findings. Forensic experts do not interpret their findings relative to the criminal investigation in which they are involved; that is the work of police investigators. The purpose of crime lab work is to provide reliable scientific analysis of evidence that can then be used in criminal investigations and, if needed later, in court proceedings.

REQUIREMENTS

High School

Almost all jobs in this field require at least a bachelor's degree. In high school, you can begin to prepare for a career in forensics by taking a heavy concentration of science courses, including chemistry, biology, physiology, and physics. Computer skills are also important, especially for fingerprint classifiers. A basic grounding in spoken and written communications will be useful because forensic experts must write very detailed reports and are sometimes called on to present their findings in court.

Postsecondary Training

Many universities and community colleges in the United States offer programs in forensic science, pathology, and various aspects of crime lab work. These courses are often spread throughout the school, in the anatomy, physiology, chemistry, or biology departments, or they may be grouped together as part of the criminal justice department.

Certification or Licensing

Certification may be an advantage for people working in toxicology and document examination. Specialists in these and other disciplines may also be required to take undergraduate and graduate course work in their areas. In a field such as toxicology, advanced chemistry work is important.

Other Requirements

To be successful in this field, you should have an aptitude for scientific investigation, an inquiring and logical mind, and the abil-

A police forensic team investigates a bomb blast site. *(Reuters/Corbis)*

ity to make precise measurements and observations. Patience and persistence are important qualities, as is a good memory. Forensic experts must constantly bear in mind that the accuracy of their lab investigations can have great consequences for others.

EXPLORING

A large community police department may have a crime lab of its own whose experts can give you specific information about their work and the preparation that helped them build their careers. Smaller communities often use the lab facilities of a larger city nearby or the state police. A school counselor or a representative of the local police may be able to help you arrange a tour of these labs. Lectures in forensic science given at universities or police conventions may also be open to students. Online services and Internet access may provide entry to forums devoted to forensic science and are good sources of information on the daily and professional experiences of people already active in this field.

EMPLOYERS

Forensic scientists are typically employed by large police departments or state law enforcement agencies nationwide. However, individuals in certain disciplines are often self-employed or work in the private sector. For example, *forensic engineers*—who use mathematical principles to reconstruct accident scenes, determine the origins of explosions and fires, or review the design of chemical or molecular structures—may be employed by large corporations, small firms, or government agencies. *Forensic anthropologists*, who identify skeletal remains, may work within a university or college, teaching related courses, conducting research, and consulting on cases submitted by law enforcement agencies. They may also be employed by the military or a medical examiner's office. Many forensic science concentrations also offer part-time or consulting opportunities, depending on an individual's level of education and experience.

STARTING OUT

Crime labs are maintained by the federal government and by state and local governments. Applications should be made directly to the personnel department of the government agency supporting the lab. Civil service appointments usually require applicants to take an examination. Such appointments are usually widely advertised well in advance of the application date. Those working for the FBI or other law enforcement agencies usually undergo background checks, which examine their character, background, previous employers, and family and friends.

ADVANCEMENT

In a large crime laboratory, forensic technicians usually advance from an assistant's position to working independently at one or more special types of analysis. From there they may advance to a position as project leader or being in charge of all aspects of one particular investigation. In smaller labs, one technician may have to fill many roles. With experience, such a technician may progress to more responsible work but receive no advancement in title. Fingerprint classifiers who work for police departments may pursue advancement with a different government agency or apply for positions with the FBI.

Crucial to advancement is further education. Forensic experts need to be familiar with scientific procedures such as gas chromatography, ultraviolet and infrared spectrophotometry, mass spectroscopy, electrophoresis, polarizing microscopy, light microscopy, and conventional and isoelectric focusing; knowledge of these analytical techniques and procedures is taught or more fully explored at the master's and doctorate levels. Other, more specific areas of forensics, such as DNA analysis, require advanced degrees in molecular biology and genetics.

EARNINGS

Earnings for forensic analysts vary with the employer, geographic location, and educational and skill levels. Salaries for entry-level positions as research assistants or technicians working in local and regional labs range from $20,000 to $25,000. For those individuals with a bachelor's degree and two to five years of specialized experience, salaries range from $30,000 to $40,000. Salaries for those with advanced degrees range from $50,000 to well over $100,000 a year. The U.S. Department of Labor reports that the median hourly salary for forensic science technicians was $21.79 in 2006. For full-time employment, this means a median salary of approximately $45,330 a year.

WORK ENVIRONMENT

Forensic experts usually perform the analytical portion of their work in clean, quiet, air-conditioned laboratories, but they are frequently required to travel to crime scenes to collect evidence or study the site to understand more fully the evidence collected by detectives. When gathering evidence and analyzing it, forensic experts need to be able to concentrate, sometimes in crowded, noisy situations. For this reason, forensic experts must be adaptable and able to work in a variety of environments, including dangerous or unpleasant places.

Many crime scenes are grisly and may be extremely distressing for beginning workers and even for more seasoned professionals. In addition, forensic experts who work with human remains will regularly view corpses, and, more often than not, these corpses will have been mutilated in some way or be in varying degrees of decomposition. Individuals interested in this field need to develop the detachment and objectivity necessary to view corpses and extract specimens for testing and analysis.

Simulating the precise conditions of a crime site for a full analysis is often crucial, so forensic experts often return to the site so that they can perform tests or functions outside of the controlled environment of their lab. When traveling to the scene of a crime, forensic experts may have to carry cases of tools, cameras, and chemicals. In order not to risk contaminating evidence, they must follow strict procedures (both in and out of the laboratory) for collecting and testing evidence; these procedures can be extremely time-consuming and thus require a great deal of patience. Forensic experts also need to be able to arrive at and present their findings impartially. In large labs, they often work as part of a team under the direction of a senior technologist. They may experience eyestrain and contact with strong chemicals, but little heavy physical work is involved.

OUTLOOK

The number of forensic experts employed in the United States is expected to grow much faster than the average for all other occupations through 2014, according to the U.S. Department of Labor. Population increases, a rising crime rate, and the greater emphasis on scientific methodology in crime investigation have increased the need for trained experts. Forensic experts who are employed by state public safety departments should experience especially strong employment opportunities, although some government agencies may be under pressure to reduce staff because of budget problems. Forensic experts with a four-year degree in forensic science will enjoy the best employment prospects.

FOR MORE INFORMATION

For information on careers and colleges and universities that offer forensic science programs, contact
American Academy of Forensic Sciences
410 North 21st Street
Colorado Springs, CO 80904-2798
Tel: 719-636-1100
http://www.aafs.org

To learn more about forensic services at the FBI, visit the FBI Laboratory Division's Web site.
Federal Bureau of Investigation (FBI)
J. Edgar Hoover Building
935 Pennsylvania Avenue, NW
Washington, DC 20535-0001
Tel: 202-324-3000
http://www.fbi.gov/hq/lab/labhome.htm

For additional information on forensics and forensics professionals, contact the following organizations:
American Society of Questioned Document Examiners
PO Box 18298
Long Beach, CA 90807-8298
http://www.asqde.org

Society of Forensic Toxicologists
One MacDonald Center
1 North MacDonald Street, Suite 15
Mesa, AZ 85201-7340
Tel: 888-866-7638
Email: office@soft-tox.org
http://www.soft-tox.org

Industrial Chemicals Workers

OVERVIEW

Industrial chemicals workers are employed in a variety of interrelated and interdependent industries and companies in which one concern often makes chemical precursors or starting materials for another's use. Most chemical workers convert the starting products or raw materials into other chemical compounds and derivative products, such as pharmaceuticals, plastics, solvents, and paints. In addition to being actively engaged in chemical operations, some workers are required to maintain safety, health, and environmental standards mandated by the federal government and perform routine and preventive maintenance tasks. Still others handle, store, and transport chemicals and operate batch processes.

HISTORY

Although its origins can be traced to ancient Greece, chemistry was recognized as a physical science during the 17th century. The alkali industry, which began then, made alkalis (caustic compounds such as sodium or potassium hydroxide) and alkaline salts such as soda ash (sodium carbonate) from wood and plant ashes. These compounds were then used to make soap and glass. By 1775, the natural sources of these alkaline compounds could not meet demand. Encouraged by the French Academy of Sciences, Nicholas Leblanc devised a synthetic process to manufacture them cheaply. Large-scale use of his process came a few years later in England. Inspired and encouraged by Leblanc's success, other

QUICK FACTS

School Subjects
Chemistry
Mathematics

Personal Skills
Following instructions
Mechanical/manipulative

Work Environment
Primarily indoors
Primarily one location

Minimum Education Level
High school diploma

Salary Range
$20,000 to $40,000 to $60,000+

Certification or Licensing
None available

Outlook
Decline

DOT
551

GOE
06.04.11

NOC
9613

O*NET-SOC
51-8091.00, 51-9011.01, 51-9011.02

scientists developed new methods for making a variety of industrially important chemicals. This marked the beginning of the modern industrial chemicals industry. In the 1880s, the Leblanc process was superseded by the Solvay process. In the industrial chemical field today, many compounds, such as ethylene, which is derived from petroleum, are used to synthesize countless other useful products. Ethylene can be used to make polyethylene, polyethylene terephthalate, polystyrene, vinyl plastics, ethyl alcohol, and ethyl ether, to name just a few. Many of these, in turn, are used in fibers, fabrics, paints, resins, fuels, and pharmaceuticals. Thus, it is evident how one industry feeds off and relies on another. New uses for chemicals continue to be found, as well as new compounds to be synthesized. Some of these compounds will eventually supplant those now in use.

THE JOB

Workers in industrial chemicals plants make all the products previously mentioned plus thousands more. Basic chemicals such as sulfuric acid, nitric acid, hydrochloric acid, sodium hydroxide, sodium chloride, and ammonia are made by giant companies. The demand for these products is so great that only large companies can afford to build the factories and buy the equipment and the raw materials to produce these chemicals at the low prices for which they sell them. On the other hand, these giant companies rarely make specialty chemicals because they either can't afford to or they don't wish to make the necessary investment due to the very limited market. Those products are made by small companies.

Because of the large variety of chemicals produced and the number of different processes involved, there are hundreds of job categories. Many of the jobs have quite a bit in common. In general, workers measure batches according to formulas; set reaction parameters for temperature, pressure, or flow of materials; and read gauges to monitor processes. They do routine testing, keep records, and may write progress reports. Many operators use computerized control panels to monitor processes. Some operate mixing machines, agitator tanks, blenders, steam cookers, and other equipment. The worker may pour two or more raw ingredients from storage vats into a reaction vessel or empty cars from overhead conveyors, dumping the contents of a barrel or drum, or manually transfer materials from a hopper, box, or other container. The worker measures a preset amount of ingredients and then activates the mixing machine, while keeping an eye on the gauges and controls.

When the mixture has reached the desired consistency, color, or other characteristic, a test sample may be removed. If the analysis

Industrial chemicals workers must be willing to do repetitive and
sometimes monotonous tasks. *(Corbis)*

is satisfactory, the mixture is moved to its next destination either
by piping, pumping into another container or processing machine,
emptying into drums or vats, or by a conveyor. The operator then
records the amount and condition of the mixture and readies his
equipment for the next run.

Other workers may separate contaminants, undesirable byproducts,
and unreacted materials with equipment that filters, strains, sifts, or
centrifuges. Filters and centrifuges are often used to separate a slurry
into liquid and solid parts. The *filter-press operator* sets up the press
by covering the filter plates with canvas or paper sheets that separate
the solids from the liquid portion. After the filtration, the plates are
removed and cleaned. The centrifuge is a machine that spins a solid-
liquid mixture like a washing machine in the spin cycle to separate
it into solid and liquid components. If the desired end product is the
liquid, the *centrifuge operator* discards the solids, and vice versa.

Distillation operators use equipment that separates liquid mixtures by first heating them to their boiling points. The heated vapors

rise into a distillation column. If a very pure liquid is desired, a fractional distillation column is used. A distillation apparatus consists of an electrically or steam-heated still pot, a distillation column, a water-cooled condenser, and a collector. In this process, the hot vapors rise through the distillation column. The condenser cools the vapors and converts them back into a liquid. The condensed liquid is collected and removed for further use. Distillation, a very important separation technique for purifying and separating liquids, is widely used in the liquor industry, petroleum refineries, and chemical companies that make and use liquid chemicals.

Solid chemical mixtures often need to be dried before they can be used. Workers heat, bake, dry, and melt chemicals with kilns, vacuum dryers, rotary or tunnel furnaces, and spray dryers. The workers who operate this equipment, regardless of the industry, perform the same operations.

The paint industry manufactures paints, varnishes, shellacs, lacquers, and a variety of liquid products for decorative and protective coatings. It not only makes many of the materials that go into its products but also purchases chemicals, resins, solvents, dyes, and pigments from others. In its operations, it performs many of the same tasks as those described. Coating and laminating are related industries. Their workers operate press rollers; laminating, coating, and printing machines; and sprayers. They carefully apply measured thicknesses of coating materials to a variety of substrates, such as paper, plastic, metal, and fabric.

REQUIREMENTS

High School

Most of the equipment in the industrial chemicals industry is now automated and computer controlled. Because of the complex equipment used, employers prefer to hire workers with at least a high school diploma. Knowledge of basic mathematics, science, and computer skills is essential for those seeking employment in this field. Machine shop experience is also useful.

Postsecondary Training

Entry-level employees always get on-the-job training and special classroom work. Classes may include heat transfer principles, the basics of distillation, how to take readings on tanks and other equipment, and how to read blueprints. Workers also get safety training about the chemicals and processes they will encounter.

More advanced knowledge of chemistry and physics is important for those who hope to advance to supervisory and managerial positions. Training to become a skilled operator may take two to five years. Information on apprenticeship programs can be found through state employment bureaus. Some community colleges offer programs that allow students to combine classroom work with on-the-job experience to enhance their skills and knowledge.

Other Requirements

Workers in this industry must be dependable, alert, accurate, and able to follow instructions exactly. They must always be mindful of the potential hazards involved in working with chemicals and cannot ever be careless. They should be conscientious, able to work without direct supervision, willing to do repetitive and sometimes monotonous work, and be able to work well with others.

EXPLORING

A helpful and inexpensive way to explore employment opportunities is to talk with someone who has worked in the industry in which you are interested. Also, it may be possible to arrange a tour of a manufacturing plant by contacting its public relations department. Another way to explore chemical manufacturing occupations is to check high school or public libraries for books on the industry. Other sources include trade journals, high school guidance counselors, and university career services offices. You should join your high school or college science clubs. You can also subscribe to the American Chemical Society's *ChemMatters,* a quarterly magazine for high school chemistry students. (To read the magazine online, visit the society's Web site, http://www.chemistry.org/portal/a/c/s/1/home. html, and click "Educators and Students.")

EMPLOYERS

Industrial chemicals workers are a necessary part of all chemical manufacturing whether the industry is producing basic chemicals, pharmaceuticals, paints, food, or a myriad of other products. The companies vary in size, depending on the nature of the products they produce. Some large industrial chemicals companies (DuPont and Dow Chemical Company, for example) may make the chemicals they use in their own operations. Others purchase what they need from specialty chemical companies, such as Mallinckrodt Baker.

Basic chemicals, such as sodium hydroxide and nitric acid, are usually made by giant companies, while small companies may make fine or specialty chemicals to supply to other manufacturers. Some of the duties are involved in the actual production process; others concern the equipment used in manufacturing; still others test finished products to ensure that they meet industry and government standards of purity and safety. There are a number of government laboratories, such as the Department of Agriculture and the National Institute of Standards and Technology, that employ chemical workers.

STARTING OUT

High school graduates qualify for entry-level factory jobs as helpers, laborers, and material movers. They learn how to handle chemicals safely and acquire skills that enable them to advance to higher levels of responsibility. Students interested in a job in the industrial chemicals industry should look for information on job openings through classified ads and employment agencies. Information can also be obtained by contacting the personnel offices of individual chemical plants and local union offices of the International Chemical Workers Union and the United Steel, Paper and Forestry, Rubber, Manufacturing, Energy, Allied-Industrial and Service Workers International Union (more commonly known as the United Steelworkers of America). High school and college guidance and career services offices are other knowledgeable sources.

ADVANCEMENT

Movement into higher paying jobs is possible with increased experience and on-the-job training. Advancement usually requires mastery of advanced skills. Employers often offer classes for those who want to improve their skills and advance their careers.

Most workers start as laborers or unskilled helpers. They can advance to mechanic and installer jobs through formal vocational or in-house training. Or they can move up to positions as skilled operators of complex processes. They may become operators who monitor the flow and mix ratio of chemicals as they go through the production process. Experienced and well-trained production workers can advance to become supervisors overseeing an entire process.

EARNINGS

In 2006, median annual earnings for chemical equipment operators and tenders were $40,290, according to the U.S. Department of Labor. Chemical plant and system operators earned median annual salaries of $49,080, while mixing and blending machine setters, operators, and tenders averaged $29,330. Managers and supervisors earn salaries that range from $50,000 to $60,000 or higher depend-

Facts About the Chemical Industry

- More than 881,000 people are employed in the chemical industry in the United States. In addition, nearly five million jobs are indirectly generated by the chemical industry.
- There are more than 15,380 chemical establishments in the United States.
- The average industry wage is $68,174.
- In 2004, 12 percent of chemical manufacturing workers were members of a union or covered by union contracts—slightly less than the average for workers in all industries.

Sources: American Chemical Society, U.S. Department of Labor

ing on job duties and the number of workers that they supervise. Workers are usually paid more for night, weekend, and overtime work. Hourly rates for each production job are often set by union contract. Fringe benefits vary among employers. They may include group, hospital, dental, and life insurance; paid holidays and vacations; and pension plans. Also, many workers qualify for college tuition aid from their companies.

WORK ENVIRONMENT

Working conditions in plants vary, depending on specific jobs, the type and condition of the equipment used, and the size and age of the plant. Chemical processing jobs used to be very dangerous, dirty, and disagreeable. However, working conditions have steadily improved over the years as a result of environmental, safety, and health standards mandated by the government. As a result of government intervention, chemical manufacturing now has an excellent safety record that is superior to other manufacturing industries. Nevertheless, chemical plants by their very nature can be extremely hazardous if strict safety procedures are not followed and enforced. Precautions include wearing protective clothing and equipment where required. Hard hats and safety goggles are worn throughout the plant.

Although few jobs in this industry are strenuous, they may become monotonous. Since manufacturing is a continuous process, most chemical plants operate around the clock. Once a process has begun, it cannot be stopped. This means that workers are needed for three shifts; split, weekend, and night shifts are common.

OUTLOOK

While the output and productivity of the industrial chemicals industry is expected to increase, the U.S. Department of Labor predicts that employment for industrial chemicals workers will decline through 2014. More efficient production processes, increased plant automation, and growing competition with overseas chemical manufacturers will limit job growth for production workers in this industry.

Advancing technology should create jobs for technical workers with the necessary skills to handle increasingly complex chemical processes and controls, as well as jobs for computer specialists who have technical expertise in computer-controlled production.

FOR MORE INFORMATION

To subscribe to ChemMatters *or to learn more about chemical process industries and technical operators, contact*

American Chemical Society
Career Education
1155 16th Street, NW
Washington, DC 20036-4801
Tel: 800-227-5558
http://www.chemistry.org

The American Chemistry Council offers a great deal of information about the chemical industry and maintains an informative Web site.

American Chemistry Council
1300 Wilson Boulevard
Arlington VA 22209-2323
Tel: 703-741-5000
http://www.americanchemistry.com

For information on chemical engineering, contact

American Institute of Chemical Engineers
3 Park Avenue
New York, NY 10016-5991
Tel: 800-242-4363
http://www.aiche.org

Industrial Safety and Health Technicians

OVERVIEW

Industrial safety and health technicians are part of a management team of an industrial plant. Their job is to make the workplace as safe as possible. Industrial safety and health technicians take direction from plant managers, industrial engineers, and government agencies to verify that machinery and the physical plant meet established safety codes. They make sure that workers understand required safety procedures, and they also work to ensure workers' compliance with these important safety measures.

HISTORY

In the 18th century, when the industrial revolution began, waterpower and steam-driven machines made mass production possible. The primary objective then was to achieve high production rates. Safety on the job was often considered the responsibility of the worker, not the employer.

By the beginning of the 20th century, working conditions had vastly improved. Workers and employers found that the cost of injuries and the loss of production and wages from industrial accidents were very expensive to both parties. Industry owners and labor leaders began to use safety-engineering methods to prevent industrial accidents and diseases.

The combined efforts of business, government, and labor organizations resulted in increased safety awareness and much safer and healthier working environments. Industrial safety engineers and industrial hygienists studied accidents and learned how to make

QUICK FACTS

School Subjects
Health
Technical/shop

Personal Skills
Helping/teaching
Leadership/management

Work Environment
Primarily indoors
Primarily one location

Minimum Education Level
Associate's degree

Salary Range
$25,240 to $42,160 to
$100,000+

Certification or Licensing
Voluntary

Outlook
About as fast as the average

DOT
168

GOE
04.04.02

NOC
2263

O*NET-SOC
17-2111.01, 29-9010.00,
29-9011.00, 29-9012.00

workplaces safer for employees, leading to the development of industrial safety standards and practices.

With the passage of the Occupational Safety and Health Act (OSHA) in 1970, highly developed and accepted standards for safety and health in the workplace became the legal responsibility of employers. Many large industrial companies with established safety programs hired safety and health technicians to make sure that their operations met OSHA requirements. Failure to meet OSHA requirements would result in fines.

After this legislation, companies large and small that had no formal safety programs hired safety professionals and enacted programs to ensure OSHA compliance. Insurance companies expanded their loss-control consulting staffs, and the number of independent safety consulting firms increased because many small businesses needed informed and reliable help to make their workplaces safe under the law.

The demand for trained safety and health personnel increased accordingly. Today, continued public support and concern for occupational safety and health has made it clear that there is a need for broadly educated, specially trained, and highly skilled industrial safety and health technicians.

THE JOB

There were 4.2 million cases of nonfatal work-related sickness or injury in the United States in 2005, according to the U.S. Bureau of Labor Statistics. About 1.2 million of these cases were serious enough to cause at least one lost workday. Many cases involve far more time lost from work and sometimes even death. In 2005, 5,734 fatal work injuries occurred. It is the task of the industrial safety and health staff, including technicians, to prevent on-the-job accidents and illnesses.

Industrial safety and health technicians work for many kinds of employers. These include manufacturing industries and businesses, construction and drilling companies, transportation, mining, and other industrial employers, and medical, educational, and scientific institutions. Experienced industrial safety and health technicians may work as instructors with programs for training safety personnel, in federal, state, and local government agencies, insurance firms, and safety consulting firms.

These technicians usually work as members of a team directed by a safety engineer or the head of the engineering department. Many times, the team works relatively independently, following safety plans drawn up by engineers or outside consultants. Depending on their backgrounds, experience, or the nature of the workplace, industrial safety and health technicians may be asked to assume responsibility for safety within a given department, a single site, or several locations.

The work of these technicians is typically a combination of three general activities. The first is to communicate safety consciousness and teach safety practices to employees. Their second duty is to perform on-the-job inspections and analyze potential safety and health hazards in the workplace. Thirdly, technicians write reports, keep records, work with engineers to design safeguards, study ways to improve safety, and communicate suggestions to supervisors.

Safety and health technicians are usually expected to work with the personnel department to organize, schedule, and conduct safety instruction sessions for new workers. Most of the instruction sessions for new employees involve orientation and tours through the areas where they will work. Tours include explanations of the safeguards, safety rules, protection systems, hazards, safety signs, and warnings. They also cover any work rules regarding safety shoes, clothing, glasses, hard hats, and other safety regulations.

These instructional duties are among the technician's most important activities. Understanding and avoiding the actions that cause injury in the first place is more effective than simply reacting to workplace illnesses and accidents after they happen.

Potential hazards in the workplace that are monitored by technicians include airborne health hazards, such as dusts, mists, fumes, and gases; physical hazards, such as noise, vibration, extreme temperatures, and pressure; and mechanical and electrical hazards such as unguarded machinery or improperly grounded or insulated equipment. Technicians also review facilities, checking working surfaces, fire protection systems, sanitation facilities, and electricity and water utilities.

More specialized tasks performed by industrial safety and health technicians cover many areas. They conduct periodic workplace investigations to discover and define substances, conditions, and activities that may contribute to the contamination of a work environment. Technicians review safety evaluation reports from state and insurance inspectors, worker committees, or management to help coordinate actions needed to correct hazards. They also inspect and maintain records on safety equipment, arranging for any necessary repairs.

Technicians may review operating, maintenance, and emergency instructions to be sure that they are adequate and timely. They assist in accident and injury investigations and maintain follow-up records to make sure that corrective actions were taken after an incident.

They recommend to their supervisors ways to improve the company's safety and health performance record and work with management to create a more effective safety policy. This may involve studying current safety reports and attending industrial safety and health conferences.

Technicians also maintain records of the company workers' compensation program and OSHA illness or injury reports. These duties are coordinated with the company's personnel and accounting departments.

In companies with large safety and health staffs, the work of technicians may be more specialized. For example, they may only conduct inspections and design safeguards to prevent accidents. In smaller companies, the beginning technician may be considered the *safety engineer,* responsible for an entire occupational safety program that has been prepared by an outside consultant.

REQUIREMENTS

High School

While in high school, take classes that will prepare you for a two-year industrial safety and health program at a technical or community college. Recommended courses include English with special emphasis on writing and speech, algebra, and science classes with laboratory study. Other valuable courses are computer science, shop, and mechanical drawing.

Postsecondary Training

A two-year program for industrial safety and health technicians involves intensive classroom study with equally intensive laboratory study. In fact, students will typically spend more time in the laboratory than the classroom.

The first year of study usually includes fundamentals of fire protection, safety and health regulations and codes, advanced first aid, and record keeping. The second year typically covers industrial chemical hazards, materials handling and storage, environmental health, sanitation and public health, and disaster preparedness.

If you plan to advance from the position of technician, a four-year degree is recommended. According to the Board of Certified Safety Professionals, more than 90 percent of those in industrial safety positions have earned a bachelor's degree. Though many major in safety, others pursue degrees in engineering, science, or business.

Certification or Licensing

The Occupational Safety and Health Administration and the American Society of Safety Engineers provide safety training programs to corporate employees and to the general public. After course completion, participants receive an official certificate.

The Board of Certified Safety Professionals offers the designation certified safety professional (CSP) to eligible candidates. Though not required, certification has many advantages. For example, a recent salary survey reported that safety professionals with the CSP designation earned 15 to 20 percent more than those who were not certified.

The American Board of Industrial Hygiene also offers the certified industrial hygienist and certified associate industrial hygienist designations. Candidates must have training and education in the field of industrial hygiene, complete an application, and pass a written examination.

Other Requirements

Physical requirements for this career include strong eyesight and adequate physical strength and coordination. Color blindness can be a limiting factor because most factories or industrial plants have color-coded wiring and piping systems. Adequate hearing is needed to interpret normal and abnormal sounds in the workplace that might indicate potential health or safety hazards.

Technicians must be able to make careful, systematic, step-by-step analyses of possible industrial accidents or illness in many different kinds of workplaces. As a result, they should be patient, detail oriented, and thorough in their work. Careful inspections protect the health and lives of hundreds of workers.

EXPLORING

To learn more about the career, talk to a career guidance counselor about your interest in the safety professions. He or she may have advice on how to research the job, visit a plant, or meet with a working industrial safety and health technician. If you live near a community college with a safety and health program, visit its career information center, library, and counseling staff to learn more about the career.

Local OSHA offices and chapters of the National Safety Council can also provide excellent information about this career. Safety publications, such as *Safety+Health* magazine (http://www.nsc.org/shnews), also provide information about occupational safety.

Summer or part-time work in manufacturing or warehousing can introduce you to the environments in which you might eventually work. Learning on-the-job safety and health rules in a factory, plant, or other workplace serves as good experience.

EMPLOYERS

According to the Board of Certified Safety Professionals, 32 percent of safety professionals are employed in manufacturing and production industries. Other safety professionals work in the construction, transportation, mining, petroleum, and medical industries. Technicians work for a wide variety of employers, large and small. At a large company, technicians are likely to be part of a large safety and health staff, with their own areas of specialization and responsibilities. At a small company, the safety and health staff may consist of just one or two technicians who assume full responsibility for the entire operation.

Most manufacturing companies have a safety officer, an industrial hygienist, or a safety engineer. In addition, many insurance companies have safety and health specialists on their staffs. Some industrial safety and health technicians work for the government, chiefly for OSHA, or as instructors at community colleges.

STARTING OUT

Many graduates of industrial safety and health technology programs find their first jobs before graduation because recruiters regularly visit schools with such programs. School career services officers identify graduating students that may be interested in jobs in industrial safety so that recruiters can interview and sometimes even make job offers on the spot. Work study arrangements can also result in placements for students after graduation.

Another method of entering a technician career is by first working as an assistant to a safety engineer or a member of the industrial safety and health staff of a large company. After gaining some experience and making contacts in the industry, a more involved job in occupational safety may become available.

Some individuals who join industrial safety and health staffs have trained in specialized work, such as arc welding, machining, foundry work, or metal forming, all of which can be especially hazardous. These experienced workers have already learned safety and health principles while on the job. With additional study, these workers can become industrial safety and health technicians in their specific fields.

ADVANCEMENT

Advancement for industrial safety and health technicians usually results from formal training and continued study. Job experience and exceptional work performance may also lead to a promotion and more responsibility. Keeping abreast of developments and safety practices can help to reduce costs, increase productivity, and improve worker morale and company image. Technicians who help make such improvements in the workplace usually receive higher status and salary with time.

Safety technicians employed by large organizations with specialized departments can work in different areas of the safety system throughout the plant. After working at various assignments, they may advance to a supervisory position overseeing multiple departments or work areas.

After several years of experience and a good record of success, technicians can become specialized safety consultants or government inspectors. Some even become private consultants to insurance companies or small businesses. Many small companies cannot afford a full-time safety engineer and instead hire a consultant to set up an industrial safety and health plan. In such cases, the chief consultant responsible for the newly enacted plan may return periodically to check that all is working and suggest changes where needed. All of these advanced positions offer independence and financial rewards for successful and responsible industrial safety and health technicians.

EARNINGS

According to the U.S. Department of Labor, the median annual salary of industrial safety and health technicians was $42,160 in 2006. The lowest 10 percent earned less than $25,240, and the highest 10 percent earned more than $68,640. In local government, safety and health technicians had mean annual earnings of $41,890.

Recent graduates in the safety sciences receive average starting salaries of $40,000 a year or more. According to a 2005 survey by *Safety+Health* magazine, nearly half of all respondents with between five and 10 years of experience reported earning between $50,000 and $79,999 annually. As they advance, top safety professionals with more than 20 years of experience can earn salaries of $100,000 or more.

Individuals in this career can expect benefits such as paid vacation, insurance, and paid holidays equal to those for other salaried employees in an organization. Some employers provide a special compensation plan for the industrial safety and health staff, including an annual bonus for measurably improving the company's safety record. In addition, technicians and other safety workers often find that employers provide liberal support for job-related study and professional programs. This may include paid memberships in professional organizations, travel, and other costs associated with attending meetings or conferences.

WORK ENVIRONMENT

Industrial safety and health technicians work either in an office or in the part of the plant for which they are responsible. Regardless of where they work, technicians must always set a good example for safety. When appropriate, they must wear safety clothes, hats, shoes, glasses, and other protective clothing, and of course, they must follow good safety practices at all times.

Technicians usually work during the day, but in plants that operate three shifts, some evening and night hours may be necessary. Jobs in mining and oil drilling may require safety technicians to be present around the clock, with "on-and-off" work shifts. Rates of pay for such situations are usually higher than for regular eight-hour shifts.

Office work usually involves reading government regulations, filing reports, maintaining records, and studying planned changes in safety procedures. Such work is likely to be fairly routine.

Whether working as part of a team of safety professionals or as part of the organization's management, industrial safety and health technicians must be able to juggle many tasks and coordinate with people in all departments. They must be able to communicate effectively with coworkers, union representatives, and supervisors. Technicians must also be effective teachers, able to impart information and instill a "safety first" attitude in others. Safe work habits are not acquired naturally. Industrial safety and health technicians who help fellow employees to work safely at their best rate of productivity can derive great satisfaction from their work.

OUTLOOK

According to the *Occupational Outlook Handbook*, employment for industrial safety and health technicians is expected to grow about as fast as the average for all occupations through 2014. While much of the demand for these technicians is created by industrial employers and their insurers, the overall demand is affected by the level of government regulation and enforcement regarding safety and health.

Over the last decade, there has been a general pullback in government regulation and spending on industrial safety and health. If this trend continues, employment levels will probably grow slowly, since approximately 40 percent of all safety specialists and technicians are employed by federal, state, and local governments.

In private industry, employment growth will be helped by the self-enforcement of company regulations and policies. Regardless of economic fluctuations, workers demanding a safe work environment will require the expertise of industrial safety and health technicians.

FOR MORE INFORMATION

For information on certification, contact
American Board of Industrial Hygiene
6015 West St. Joseph, Suite 102
Lansing, MI 48917-3980
Tel: 517-321-2638
Email: abih@abih.org
http://www.abih.org

For information on careers and training programs, contact
American Society of Safety Engineers
1800 East Oakton Street
Des Plaines, IL 60018-2100
Tel: 847-699-2929
Email: customerservice@asse.org
http://www.asse.org

For information on certification and to download copies of the
Career Guide to the Safety Profession *and* Career Paths in Safety,
visit the BCSP Web site.
Board of Certified Safety Professionals (BCSP)
208 Burwash Avenue
Savoy, IL 61874-9571
Tel: 217-359-9263
Email: bcsp@bcsp.org
http://www.bcsp.com

For information on industrial safety issues, contact
Occupational Safety and Health Administration
U.S. Department of Labor
200 Constitution Avenue, NW
Washington, DC 20210-0001
Tel: 800-321-6742
http://www.osha.gov

For a variety of resources about industrial safety, contact
Industrial Accident Prevention Association
The Centre for Health & Safety Innovation
5110 Creekbank Road, Suite 300
Mississauga, ON L4W 0A1 Canada
Tel: 800-406-4272
http://www.iapa.on.ca

Laboratory Testing Technicians

QUICK FACTS

School Subjects
Chemistry
Physics

Personal Skills
Following instructions
Technical/scientific

Work Environment
Primarily indoors
Primarily one location

Minimum Education Level
High school diploma

Salary Range
$21,830 to $32,840 to
$50,250+

Certification or Licensing
Voluntary (certification)
Required by certain states
(licensing)

Outlook
About as fast as the average

DOT
019, 022, 078

GOE
02.05.01, 02.05.02

NOC
2211

O*NET-SOC
19-4021.00, 19-4031.00,
19-4041.00, 29-2012.00

OVERVIEW

Laboratory testing technicians conduct tests on countless substances and products. Their laboratory duties include measuring and evaluating materials and running quality control tests. They work in a variety of unrelated fields, such as medicine, metallurgy, manufacturing, geology, and meteorology. Therefore, students interested in a career as a laboratory testing technician should look for job titles such as metallurgical, medical, or pharmaceutical technicians.

HISTORY

The occupation of laboratory testing technicians goes back almost to prehistoric times when humans first learned to convert earth-derived materials into tools, weapons, and medicines. Similarly, the early alchemists who experimented with various combinations of elements set the stage for the careers of the modern day laboratory testing technician.

The career of laboratory testing technician really began with the onset of the industrial revolution. As production increased and technology became a large part of the new manufacturing processes, more and more laboratory technicians were hired to test products to make sure they met performance standards. They were often required to help design new products.

THE JOB

Laboratory testing technicians usually assist scientists in conducting tests on many substances and products. They are trained to use the required tools and instruments. Those who serve as *quality control technicians* test products to see that they are safe to use and meet performance specifications. Most of these technicians either work for testing laboratories or in research and development centers. They may test toys for safety by looking for small, separable parts, sharp edges, and fragility. Or they may test electric toasters for correct wiring, tendency to smoke or spark, and for proper grounding. In short, laboratory testing technicians in quality control are responsible for certifying that a product or material will perform according to specifications.

Not only do technicians test new products for safety and durability but they also perform failure analyses to determine the cause of the problem and how it can be prevented. Technicians also evaluate incoming materials, such as metals, ceramics, and chemicals, before they are used to verify that their suppliers have shipped the specified products. *Materials technicians* prepare specimens, set up equipment, run heating and cooling tests, and record test results. These tests are designed to determine how a certain alloy functions in a variety of test conditions. Not only do these technicians work with the test materials, they also assess the equipment used to perform the tests. For example, a technician may run tests to determine the proper temperature settings for a furnace. Some technicians may oversee the work of others to see if they are doing their assignments correctly.

Those who work in the medical field are called *medical technicians, medical laboratory technicians,* or *clinical technicians.* They work in hospitals, universities, doctors' offices, and research laboratories. They set up equipment and perform tests on body fluids, tissues, and cells; perform blood counts; and identify parasites and bacteria. Medical technicians also work in veterinary and pharmaceutical laboratories.

Some *geological technicians* test shale, sand, and other earthen materials to find the petroleum and/or mineral content. Tests are run on core samples during oil well drilling to determine what's present in the well bore. Technicians who specialize in testing ores and minerals for metal content are called *assayers.*

Regardless of the specific nature of the tests conducted by technicians, they must always keep detailed records of every step. Laboratory technicians often do a great deal of writing and must make charts, graphs, and other displays to illustrate results. They may be called on to interpret test results, to draw overall conclusions, and to make recommendations. Occasionally, laboratory testing technicians are asked to appear as witnesses in court to explain why a product failed and who may be at fault.

REQUIREMENTS

High School

If working as a laboratory testing technician sounds interesting to you, you can prepare for this work by taking at least two years of mathematics and a year each of chemistry and physics in high school. You should also consider taking shop classes to become accustomed to working with tools and to develop manual dexterity. Classes in English and writing will provide you with good experience doing research and writing reports. Take computer classes so that you become familiar with using this tool. If you know of a specific area that you want to specialize in, such as geology or medicine, you will benefit by taking relevant courses, such as earth science or biology.

Postsecondary Training

A high school diploma is the minimum requirement for finding work as a laboratory testing technician. However, a two-year associate's degree in engineering or medical technology or metallurgy—depending on the field you want to specialize in—is highly recommended. Many community colleges or technical schools offer two-year degree programs in a specific technology. Completing the associate's degree will greatly enhance your resume, help you in finding full-time positions, and allow you to advance rapidly in your field. Some technicians, such as medical technicians, may also receive appropriate training through the armed forces or through hospital certification programs.

Certification or Licensing

Depending on what type of laboratory technician you want to be, you may need certification or licensing. For example, certification for those who work as medical technicians is voluntary. However, it is highly recommended and some employers may even require it. Organizations offering certification include the American Medical Technologists, the American Association of Bioanalysts, and the Board of Registry of the American Society for Clinical Pathology, and the National Credentialing Agency for Laboratory Personnel. In addition, a number of states require that laboratory workers be licensed. Check with your state's occupational licensing board to find out specific requirements for your area. In addition, make sure any program or community college you are considering attending will provide the courses and experience you need for licensing.

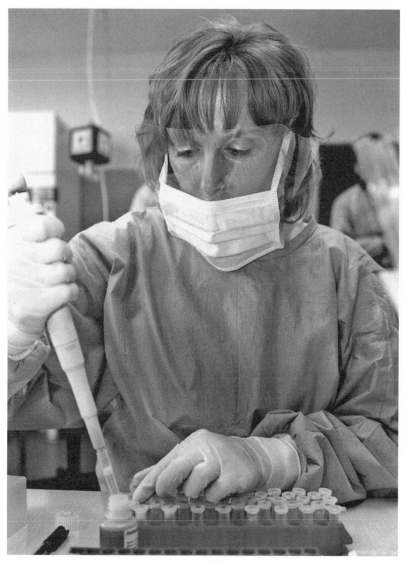

A laboratory technician tests samples for evidence of bovine spongiform encephalopathy, more commonly known as Mad Cow Disease. *(Andreas Wrede, Visum, The Image Works)*

Other Requirements

Laboratory technicians should be detail oriented and enjoy figuring out how things work. They should like problem solving and trouble shooting. For example, if you enjoy disassembling and reassembling your bicycle or tinkering with your car stereo, you will probably enjoy being a laboratory testing technician. Laboratory technicians must have the patience to repeat a test many times, perhaps even on the same material. They must be able to follow directions carefully but also should be independent and motivated to work on their own until their assigned tasks are completed.

EXPLORING

Due to the precision and training required in the field, it is unlikely that as a high school student you will be able to find a part-time or summer job as a laboratory testing technician. However, you can explore the career by contacting local technical colleges and arranging to speak with a professor in the school's technician program. Ask about the required classes, the opportunities available in your area, and any other questions you have. Through this connection you may also be able to contact a graduate of the program and arrange for an informational interview with him or her. Although you probably won't be able to get work as a laboratory testing technician at this point, some research companies and plants do offer summer jobs to high school students to work in their offices or mail rooms. While these jobs do not offer hands-on technical experience, they do allow you to experience the work environment.

EMPLOYERS

Laboratory technicians are employed in almost every type of manufacturing industry that employs chemists or chemical engineers. They are needed wherever testing is carried on, whether it is for developing new products or improving current manufacturing procedures or for quality control purposes. They are employed by such companies as Baxter, Heinz, Shell, and Eastman Kodak. They also can find positions in research institutions and in government laboratories, such as those run by the federal Departments of Health, Agriculture, and Commerce. They may assist biochemists, metallurgists, meteorologists, geologists, or other scientific personnel in large and small laboratories located all over the country.

STARTING OUT

Technical schools often help place graduating technicians. Many laboratories contact these schools directly looking for student employees or interns. Students can also contact local manufacturing companies and laboratories to find out about job openings in their area. Technicians often begin as trainees who are supervised by more experienced workers. As they gain experience, technicians take on more responsibilities and are allowed to work more independently.

ADVANCEMENT

Skilled laboratory technicians may be promoted to manager or supervisor of a division in their company. For example, a quality-control technician who has become an expert in testing computer monitors may be put in charge of others who perform this task. This supervisor may assign project duties and organize how and when results will be recorded and analyzed, and may also help other technicians solve problems they encounter when running tests. Experienced technicians may form their own testing laboratories or return to school to become engineers, physicists, or geologists.

EARNINGS

Earnings for laboratory testing technicians vary based on the type of work they do, their education and experience, and even the size of the laboratory and its location. For example, the U.S. Department of Labor reported that in 2006 the median annual earnings of medical and clinical laboratory technicians were $32,840. Salaries ranged from less than $21,830 to $50,250 or more annually. Geological and petroleum technicians had median earnings of $46,160 in 2006.

Salaries increase as technicians gain experience and as they take on supervisory responsibility. Most companies that employ laboratory testing technicians offer medical benefits, sick leave, and vacation time. However, these benefits will depend on the individual employer.

WORK ENVIRONMENT

Laboratory testing technicians typically work a 40-hour week. During especially busy times or in special circumstances, they may be required to work overtime. Most technicians work in clean, well-lighted laboratories where attention is paid to neatness and organization. Some laboratory testing technicians have their own offices, while others work in large single-room laboratories.

Some technicians may be required to go outside their laboratories to collect samples of materials for testing at locations that can be hot, cold, wet, muddy, or uncomfortable.

OUTLOOK

Overall, employment for laboratory workers is expected to grow about as fast as the average for all occupations through 2014. Environmental concerns and dwindling natural resources are causing many manufacturers to look for better ways to develop ores, minerals, and other substances from the earth. Laboratory technicians will be needed to test new production procedures as well as prototypes of new products.

Some specialties may face growth that is slightly slower than the average; for example, those who work with stone, clay, glass, fabricated metal products, and transportation equipment may experience this slow growth.

Faster-than-average employment growth is expected for medical and clinical technicians. Employment possibilities at testing laboratories will be affected by advances in technology. New testing procedures that are developed will lead to an increase in the testing that is done. However, increased automation will mean each technician can complete more work.

Technicians in any specialty who have strong educational backgrounds, keep up with developing technologies, and demonstrate knowledge of testing equipment will have the best employment opportunities.

FOR MORE INFORMATION

This organization has information on certification for medical laboratory technicians.

American Association of Bioanalysts
906 Olive Street, Suite 1200
St. Louis, MO 63101-1434
Tel: 314-241-1445
Email: aab@aab.org
http://www.aab.org

The ACS provides career information and has information on new developments in the field.

American Chemical Society (ACS)
1155 16th Street, NW
Washington, DC 20036-4801
Tel: 800-227-5558
http://www.chemistry.org

Contact this organization for certification information.
American Medical Technologists
10700 West Higgins Road
Rosemont, IL 60018-3707
Tel: 847-823-5169
Email: mail@amt1.com
http://www.amt1.com

For information on certification specialties, contact
American Society for Clinical Pathology
33 West Monroe, Suite 1600
Chicago, IL 60603-5308
Tel: 312-541-4999
Email: info@ascp.org
http://www.ascp.org

For information on certification, contact
National Credentialing Agency for Laboratory Personnel
PO Box 15945-289
Lenexa, KS 66285
Tel: 913-895-4613
Email: nca-info@goamp.com
http://www.nca-info.org

This society offers student membership and provides industry news.
The Minerals, Metals, and Materials Society
184 Thorn Hill Road
Warrendale, PA 15086-7514
Tel: 800-759-4867
Email: tmsgeneral@tms.org
http://www.tms.org

Medical Laboratory Technicians

QUICK FACTS

School Subjects
Biology
Chemistry

Personal Skills
Following instructions
Technical/scientific

Work Environment
Primarily indoors
Primarily one location

Minimum Education Level
Some postsecondary training

Salary Range
$21,830 to $32,840 to
$50,250+

Certification or Licensing
Required by certain states

Outlook
Faster than the average

DOT
078

GOE
14.05.01

NOC
3212

O*NET-SOC
29-2012.00

OVERVIEW

Medical laboratory technicians, also known as *clinical laboratory technicians*, perform routine tests in medical laboratories. These tests help physicians and other professional medical personnel diagnose and treat disease. Technicians prepare samples of body tissue; perform laboratory tests, such as urinalysis and blood counts; and make chemical and biological analyses of cells, tissue, blood, or other body specimens. They usually work under the supervision of a medical technologist or a laboratory director. Medical laboratory technicians may work in many fields, or specialize in one specific medical area, such as cytology (the study of cells), hematology (the study of blood, especially on the cellular level), serology (the study and identification of antibodies found in the blood), or histology (the study of body tissue). There are approximately 302,000 medical laboratory technicians and technologists employed in the United States.

HISTORY

Medical laboratory technology shares many important milestones with the history of medicine itself. For instance, both fields can claim as their founder Aristotle, the father of biology and physiology. Some significant achievements include Jan Swammerdam's discovery of red blood corpuscles in 1658; Anton van Leeuwenhoek's observation of microorganisms through the microscope during the latter part of the 17th century; and the discoveries of Robert Koch and Louis Pasteur in bacteriology in the 1870s.

The valuable information gained through these efforts showed medical professionals many possibilities for therapy, especially in the medical specialties of bacteriology (the study of microorganisms in the human body), cytology, histology, and hematology. The growth of these medical specialties created a steadily increasing need for laboratory personnel.

Because of the great medical advances of the 20th century, physicians are even more dependent on laboratory procedures and personnel for assistance in diagnosing and treating disease. In the early part of this century, individual physicians often taught their assistants how to perform some of the laboratory procedures frequently employed in their practices. Because the quality of work done by these technicians varied considerably, many physicians and medical educators became concerned with the problem of ensuring that assistants did the highest-quality work possible. In 1936, one of the first attempts was made to standardize the training programs for the preparation of skilled assistants—in that case, the training of medical technologists. Since then, the National Accrediting Agency for Clinical Laboratory Sciences, in association with the Commission on Accreditation of Allied Health Education Programs (CAA-HEP), has instituted standards of training for medical laboratory technicians. CAAHEP accredits educational programs offered in community, junior, and technical colleges for the training of medical laboratory technicians, and other accrediting agencies have also entered the field. For example, the Accrediting Bureau of Health Education Schools accredits education programs for medical laboratory technicians and medical assistants. In addition, CAAHEP and other agencies have accredited dozens of other programs for students willing to concentrate their studies in a medical laboratory specialty such as cytology, histology, or blood bank technology.

THE JOB

Medical laboratory technicians may be generalists in the field of laboratory technology; that is, they may be trained to carry out many different kinds of medical laboratory work. Alternatively, they may specialize in one type of medical laboratory work, such as cytology, hematology, blood bank technology, serology, or histology. The following paragraphs describe the work of generalists and those in the specialty fields of cytology, histology, and blood bank technology.

Medical laboratory technicians who work as generalists perform a wide variety of tests and laboratory procedures in chemistry, hematology, urinalysis, blood banking, serology, and microbiology. By performing these tests and procedures, they help to develop vital data on the blood, tissues, and fluids of the human body. This data is then used by physicians, surgeons, pathologists, and other medical personnel to diagnose and treat patients.

The tests and procedures that these technicians perform are more complex than the routine duties assigned to laboratory assistants, but do not require specialized knowledge like those performed by more highly trained medical technologists. In general, medical laboratory technicians work with only limited supervision. This means that while the tests they perform may have well-established procedures, the technicians themselves must exercise independent judgment. For instance, they must be able to discriminate between very similar colors or shapes, correct their own errors using established strategies, and monitor ongoing quality control measures.

To carry out these responsibilities, medical laboratory technicians need a sound knowledge of specific techniques and instruments and must be able to recognize factors that potentially influence both the procedures they use and the results they obtain.

In their work, medical laboratory technicians frequently handle test tubes and other glassware and use precision equipment, such as microscopes and automated blood analyzers. (Blood analyzers determine the levels of certain blood components like cholesterol, sugar, and hemoglobin.) Technicians also are often responsible for making sure machines are functioning and supplies are adequately stocked.

Medical laboratory technicians who specialize in cytology are usually referred to as *cytotechnicians*. Cytotechnicians prepare and stain body cell samplings using special dyes that accentuate the delicate patterns of the cytoplasm, and structures such as the nucleus. Mounted on slides, the various features of the specimen then stand out brightly under a microscope. Using microscopes that magnify cells perhaps 1,000 times, cytotechnicians screen out normal samplings and set aside those with minute irregularities (in cell size, shape, and color) for further study by a pathologist.

Medical laboratory technicians specializing in histology are usually referred to as *histologic technicians* or *tissue technicians*. Histology is the study of the structure and chemical composition of the tissues, and histologic technicians are mainly concerned with detecting tissue abnormalities and assisting in determining appropriate treatments for the disease conditions associated with the abnormalities.

Medical laboratory technicians who specialize in blood bank technology perform a wide variety of routine tests related to running

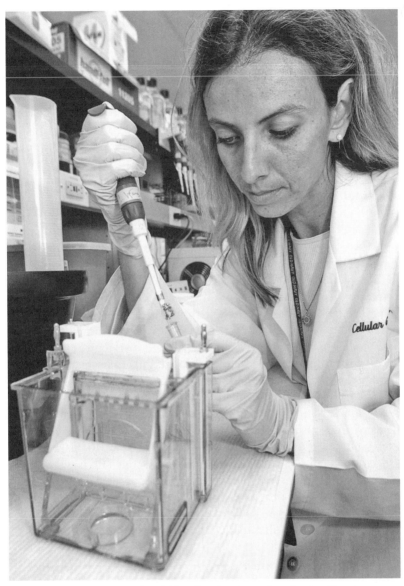

Laboratory technicians should be detail oriented and enjoy figuring out how things work. *(Peter Hvizdak, The Image Works)*

blood banks, offering transfusion services, and investigating blood diseases and reactions to transfusions. Examples of tasks frequently performed by medical laboratory technicians specializing in this field include donor screening, determining blood types, performing tests of patients' blood counts, and assisting physicians in the care of patients with blood-related problems.

REQUIREMENTS

High School

To be hired as a medical laboratory technician, you must have a high school diploma and one or two years of postsecondary training. No specific kind of high school training is required; however, you must be able to meet the admissions requirements of institutions offering post-high school training. In general, courses in biology, chemistry, mathematics, English, and computer science will be most helpful in a career as a medical laboratory technician.

Postsecondary Training

After high school, prospective technicians enroll in one- or two-year training programs accredited by the Commission on Accreditation of Allied Health Education Programs, the Accrediting Bureau of Health Education Schools, or the National Accrediting Agency for Clinical Laboratory Sciences, which fully accredits more than 465 programs. One-year programs include both classroom work and practical laboratory training and focus on areas such as medical ethics and conduct, medical terminology, basic laboratory solutions and media, manipulation of cytological and histological specimens, blood collecting techniques, and introductions to basic hematology, serology, blood banking, and urinalysis.

To earn an associate's degree, you must complete a two-year post-high school program. Like certificate programs, associate's degree programs include classroom instruction and practical training. Courses are taught both on campus and in local hospitals. On-campus courses focus on general knowledge and basic skills in laboratory testing associated with hematology, serology, chemistry, microbiology, and other pertinent biological and medical areas. The clinical training program focuses on basic principles and skills required in medical diagnostic laboratory testing.

Certification or Licensing

Students who have earned an associate's degree are eligible for certification from several different agencies, including the Board of Registry of the American Society for Clinical Pathology, the American Medical Technologists, the National Credentialing Agency for Laboratory Personnel, and the American Association of Bioanalysts.

Prospective medical laboratory technicians who think they might want to specialize in cytology or blood bank technology should definitely consider the two-year program, which will best prepare them for the additional education they may need later.

In addition to completing the educational programs described above, prospective technicians need to pass an examination after graduation to receive certification. In some states, this certificate is all that is required for employment. In other states, state licensure is also required. School officials are the best source of information regarding state requirements.

Other Requirements

Besides fulfilling the academic requirements, medical laboratory technicians must have good manual dexterity, normal color vision, the ability to follow instructions, and a tolerance for working under pressure.

EXPLORING

It is difficult for people interested in a career in medical laboratory technology to gain any direct experience through part-time employment. There are some other ways, however, to learn more about this career on a firsthand basis. Perhaps the best way is to arrange a visit to a hospital, blood bank, or commercial medical laboratory to see technicians at work at their jobs. Another way to learn about this kind of work in general, and about the training required in particular, is to visit an accredited school of medical laboratory technology to discuss career plans with the admissions counselor at the school. You can also write to the sources listed at the end of this article for more reading material on medical laboratory technology or visit their Web sites. Finally, you should remember that high school science courses with laboratory sections will give you exposure to some of the kinds of work you might do later in your career.

EMPLOYERS

Medical laboratory technicians are employed where physicians work, such as in hospitals, clinics, offices of physicians, blood blanks, and commercial medical laboratories. Approximately 302,000 medical laboratory technicians and technologists are employed in the United States, with more than half working in hospitals.

STARTING OUT

Graduates of medical laboratory technology schools usually receive assistance from faculty and school career services offices to find their first jobs. Hospitals, laboratories, and other facilities employing medical laboratory technicians may notify local schools of job openings. Often the hospital or laboratory at which you receive your practical training will offer full-time employment after graduation. Positions may also be secured using the various registries of certified medical laboratory workers. Newspaper job advertisements and commercial placement agencies are other sources of help in locating employment.

ADVANCEMENT

Medical laboratory technicians often advance by returning to school to earn a bachelor's degree. This can lead to positions as medical technologists, histological technologists, cytotechnologists, or specialists in blood bank technology.

Other technicians advance by gaining more responsibility while retaining the title of technician. For instance, with experience, these workers can advance to supervisory positions or other positions assigning work to be done by other medical laboratory workers. Medical laboratory technicians may also advance by training to do very specialized or complex laboratory or research work.

EARNINGS

Salaries of medical laboratory technicians vary according to employer and geographical area. According to the U.S. Department of Labor, median annual earnings of medical and clinical laboratory technicians were $32,840 in 2006. Salaries ranged from less than $21,830 to more than $50,250. Fifty percent of workers in this field earned between $26,430 and $41,020 annually in 2006. Medical laboratory technicians who go on to earn their bachelor's degrees and certification as medical technologists can expect an increase in annual earnings.

Most medical laboratory technicians receive paid vacations and holidays, sick leave, health insurance, and retirement benefits.

WORK ENVIRONMENT

Medical laboratory technicians work in clean, well-lit, and usually air-conditioned settings. There may, however, be unpleasant odors and some infectious materials involved in the work. In general, there are few hazards associated with these odors and materials as long as proper methods of sterilization and handling of specimens, materials, and equipment are used.

Medical laboratory technicians often spend much of their days standing or sitting on stools. A 40-hour, five-day week is normal, although those working in hospitals can expect some evening and weekend work.

Medical laboratory technicians derive satisfaction from knowing their work is very important to patients and their physicians. Although the work involves new patient samples, it also involves some very repetitive tasks that some people may find trying. Additionally, the work must often be done under time pressure, even though it is often very painstaking.

Another factor that aspiring medical laboratory technicians should keep in mind is that advancement opportunities are limited, although they do exist. To maximize their chances for advancement, medical laboratory technicians must consider getting additional training.

OUTLOOK

The U.S. Department of Labor predicts that employment for medical laboratory technicians will grow faster than the average for all occupations through 2014. Competition for jobs, however, may be strong. One reason for this increased competition is the overall national effort to control health care costs. Hospitals, where most medical laboratory technicians are employed, will seek to control costs in part through cutting down on the amount of laboratory testing they do and, consequently, the personnel they require.

Despite such cutbacks, though, the overall amount of medical laboratory testing will probably increase, as much of medical practice today relies on high-quality laboratory testing. However, because of the increased use of automation, this increase in laboratory testing probably will not lead to an equivalent growth in employment.

One other technological factor that will influence employment in this field is the development of laboratory-testing equipment that is easier to use. This means that some testing that formerly had to be done in hospitals can now be done in physicians' offices and other non-hospital settings. This development will slow growth in hospital laboratory employment; however, it should increase the number of technicians hired by medical groups and clinics, medical and diagnostic laboratories, and other ambulatory health care services such as blood and organ banks. In addition, equipment that is easier to use may also lead to technicians being able to do more kinds of testing, including some tests that used to be done only by medical technologists.

Despite these growth projections, aspiring technicians should keep in mind that medical laboratory testing is an essential element in today's medicine. For well-trained technicians who are flexible in accepting responsibilities and willing to continue their education throughout their careers, employment opportunities should remain good.

FOR MORE INFORMATION

For information on accreditation and testing, contact
Accrediting Bureau of Health Education Schools
7777 Leesburg Pike, Suite 314-North
Falls Church, VA 22043-2411
Tel: 703-917-9503
Email: info@abhes.org
http://www.abhes.org

For information on certification, contact
American Association of Bioanalysts
906 Olive Street, Suite 1200
St. Louis, MO 63101-1434
Tel: 314-241-1445
Email: aab@aab.org
http://www.aab.org

For career and certification information, contact
American Medical Technologists
10700 West Higgins Road
Rosemont, IL 60018-3707
Tel: 847-823-5169
Email: mail@amt1.com
http://www.amt1.com

For information on clinical laboratory careers and certification, contact
American Society for Clinical Laboratory Science
6701 Democracy Boulevard, Suite 300
Bethesda, MD 20817-7500
Tel: 301-657-2768
http://www.ascls.org

For information on certification, contact
American Society for Clinical Pathology
33 West Monroe, Suite 1600
Chicago IL 60603-5308
Tel: 312-541-4999
Email: info@ascp.org
http://www.ascp.org

For information on accredited programs, contact
Commission on Accreditation of Allied Health Education Programs
1361 Park Street
Clearwater, FL 33756-6039
Tel: 727-210-2350
Email: mail@caahep.org
http://www.caahep.org

For information on certification, contact
National Credentialing Agency for Laboratory Personnel
PO Box 15945-289
Lenexa, KS 66285-5945
Tel: 913-895-4613
Email: nca-info@goamp.com
http://www.nca-info.org

Petroleum Engineers

QUICK FACTS

School Subjects
Mathematics
Physics

Personal Skills
Helping/teaching
Technical/scientific

Work Environment
Indoors and outdoors
One location with some
travel

Minimum Education Level
Bachelor's degree

Salary Range
$61,516 to $108,742 to
$121,201+

Certification or Licensing
Required for certain positions

Outlook
Decline

DOT
010

GOE
02.07.04

NOC
2145

O*NET-SOC
17-2171.00

OVERVIEW

Petroleum engineers apply the principles of geology, physics, and the engineering sciences to the recovery, development, and processing of petroleum. As soon as an exploration team has located an area that could contain oil or gas, petroleum engineers begin their work, which includes determining the best location for drilling new wells, as well as the economic feasibility of developing them. They are also involved in operating oil and gas facilities, monitoring and forecasting reservoir performance, and utilizing enhanced oil recovery techniques that extend the life of wells. There are approximately 16,000 petroleum engineers employed in the United States.

HISTORY

Within a broad perspective, the history of petroleum engineering can be traced back hundreds of millions of years to when the remains of plants and animals blended with sand and mud and transformed into rock. It is from this ancient underground rock that petroleum is taken, for the organic matter of the plants and animals decomposed into oil during these millions of years and accumulated into pools deep underground.

In primitive times, people did not know how to drill for oil; instead, they collected the liquid substance after it had seeped to above-ground surfaces. Petroleum is known to have been used at that time for caulking ships and for concocting medicines.

Petroleum engineering as we know it today was not established until the mid-1800s, an incredibly long time after the fundamental ingredients of petroleum were deposited within the earth. In 1859, the American Edwin Drake was the first person to ever pump the so-called rock oil from under the ground, an endeavor that, before its success, was laughed at and considered impossible. Forward-thinking investors, however, had believed in the operation and thought that underground oil could be used as inexpensive fluid for lighting lamps and for lubricating machines (and therefore could make them rich). The drilling of the first well, in Titusville, Pennsylvania (1869), ushered in a new worldwide era: the oil age.

At the turn of the century, petroleum was being distilled into kerosene, lubricants, and wax. Gasoline was considered a useless by-product and was run off into rivers as waste. However, this changed with the invention of the internal combustion engine and the automobile. By 1915 there were more than half a million cars in the United States, virtually all of them powered by gasoline.

Edwin Drake's drilling operation struck oil 70 feet below the ground. Since that time, technological advances have been made, and the professional field of petroleum engineering has been established. Today's operations drill as far down as six miles. Because the United States began to rely so much on oil, the country contributed significantly to creating schools and educational programs in this engineering discipline. The world's first petroleum engineering curriculum was devised in the United States in 1914. Today there are fewer than 30 U.S. universities that offer petroleum engineering degrees.

The first schools were concerned mainly with developing effective methods of locating oil sites and with devising efficient machinery for drilling wells. Over the years, as sites have been depleted, engineers have been more concerned with formulating methods for extracting as much oil as possible from each well. Today's petroleum engineers focus on issues such as computerized drilling operations; however, because usually only about 40 to 60 percent of each site's oil is extracted, engineers must still deal with designing optimal conditions for maximum oil recovery.

THE JOB

Petroleum engineer is a rather generalized title that encompasses several specialties, each one playing an important role in ensuring the safe and productive recovery of oil and natural gas. In general, petroleum engineers are involved in the entire process of oil recovery, from preliminary steps, such as analyzing cost factors, to the last stages, such as monitoring the production rate and then repacking the well after it has been depleted.

Petroleum engineering is closely related to the separate engineering discipline of geoscience engineering. Before petroleum engineers can begin work on an oil reservoir, prospective sites must be sought by *geological engineers*, along with *geologists* and *geophysicists*. These scientists determine whether a site has potential oil. Petroleum engineers develop plans for drilling. Drilling is usually unsuccessful, with eight out of 10 test wells being "dusters" (dry wells) and only one of the remaining two test wells having enough oil to be commercially producible. When a significant amount of oil is discovered, engineers can begin their work of maximizing oil production at the site. The development company's *engineering manager* oversees the activities of the various petroleum engineering specialties, including reservoir engineers, drilling engineers, and production engineers.

Reservoir engineers use the data gathered by the previous geoscience studies and estimate the actual amount of oil that will be extracted from the reservoir. Reservoir engineers determine whether the oil will be taken by primary methods (simply pumping the oil from the field) or by enhanced methods (using additional energy such as water pressure to force the oil up). The reservoir engineer is responsible for calculating the cost of the recovery process relative to the expected value of the oil produced and simulates future performance using sophisticated computer models. Besides performing studies of existing company-owned oil fields, reservoir engineers also evaluate fields the company is thinking of buying.

Drilling engineers work with geologists and drilling contractors to design and supervise drilling operations. They are the engineers involved with the actual drilling of the well. They ask: What will be the best methods for penetrating the earth? It is the responsibility of these workers to supervise the building of the derrick (a platform, constructed over the well, that holds the hoisting devices), choose the equipment, and plan the drilling methods. Drilling engineers must have a thorough understanding of the geological sciences so that they can know, for instance, how much stress to place on the rock being drilled.

Production engineers determine the most efficient methods and equipment to optimize oil and gas production. For example, they establish the proper pumping unit configuration and perform tests to determine well fluid levels and pumping load. They plan field workovers and well stimulation techniques such as secondary and tertiary recovery (for example, injecting steam, water, or a special recovery fluid) to maximize field production.

Various research personnel are involved in this field; some are more specialized than others. They include the *research chief engineer*, who directs studies related to the design of new drilling and production methods, the *oil-well equipment research engineer,* who directs research to design improvements in oil-well machinery and devices, and the *oil-field equipment test engineer,* who conducts experiments to determine the effectiveness and safety of these improvements.

In addition to all of the above, sales personnel play an important part in the petroleum industry. *Oil-well equipment and services sales engineers* sell various types of equipment and devices used in all stages of oil recovery. They provide technical support and service to their clients, including oil companies and drilling contractors.

REQUIREMENTS

High School

In high school, you can prepare for college engineering programs by taking courses in mathematics, physics, chemistry, geology, and computer science. Economics, history, and English are also highly recommended because these subjects will improve your communication and management skills. Mechanical drawing and foreign languages are also helpful.

Postsecondary Training

A bachelor's degree in engineering is the minimum requirement. In college, you can follow either a specific petroleum engineering curriculum or a program in a closely related field, such as geophysics or mining engineering. In the United States, there are fewer than 30 universities and colleges that offer programs that concentrate on petroleum engineering, many of which are located in California and Texas. The first two years toward the bachelor of science degree involve the study of many of the same subjects taken in high school, only at an advanced level, as well as basic engineering courses. In the junior and senior years, students take more specialized courses: geology, formation evaluation, properties of reservoir rocks and fluids, well drilling, properties of reservoir fluids, petroleum production, and reservoir analysis.

Because the technology changes so rapidly, many petroleum engineers continue their education to receive a master's degree and then a doctorate. Petroleum engineers who have earned advanced degrees command higher salaries and often are eligible for better advancement opportunities. Those who work in research and teaching positions are usually required to have these higher credentials.

Students considering an engineering career in the petroleum industry should be aware that the industry uses all kinds of engineers. People with chemical, electrical, geoscience, mechanical, environmental, and other engineering degrees are also employed in this field.

Mean Annual Earnings by Specialty, 2006

Architectural, engineering, and related services	$112,310
Oil and gas extraction	$112,200
Pipeline transportation of crude oil	$101,610
Petroleum and coal products manufacturing	$100,400
Management, scientific, and technical consulting services	$94,790
Support activities for mining	$87,140

Source: U.S. Department of Labor

Certification or Licensing

Many jobs, especially public projects, require that the engineer be licensed as a professional engineer (P.E.). To be licensed, candidates must have a degree from an engineering program accredited by the Accreditation Board for Engineering and Technology. Additional requirements for obtaining the license vary from state to state, but all applicants must take an exam and have several years of related experience on the job or in teaching. For more information on licensing and examination requirements, visit http://www.ncees.org.

Other Requirements

Students thinking about this career should enjoy science and math. You need to be a creative problem-solver who likes to come up with new ways to get things done and try them out. You need to be curious, wanting to know why and how things are done. You also need to be a logical thinker with a capacity for detail, and you must be a good communicator who can work well with others.

EXPLORING

One of the most satisfying ways to explore this occupation is to participate in Junior Engineering Technical Society (JETS) programs. JETS participants enter engineering design and problem-solving contests and learn team development skills, often with an engineering mentor. Science fairs and clubs also offer fun and challenging ways to learn about engineering.

Certain students are able to attend summer programs held at colleges and universities that focus on material not traditionally offered in high school. Usually these programs include recreational activities such as basketball, swimming, and track and field. For example, Worcester Polytechnic Institute offers the Frontiers program, a two-week residential session for high school seniors. For more information, visit http://www.admissions.wpi.edu/Frontiers. The American Indian Science and Engineering Society (AISES) also sponsors two- to six-week mathematics and science camps that are open to Native American students and held at various college campuses. For more information, visit http://www.aises.org.

Talking with someone who has worked as a petroleum engineer is also a very helpful and inexpensive way to explore this field. One good way to find an experienced person to talk to is through Internet sites that feature career areas to explore, industry message boards, and mailing lists.

You can also explore this career by touring oilfields or corporate sites (contact the public relations department of oil companies for more information), or you can try to land a temporary or summer job in the petroleum industry on a drilling and production crew. Trade journals, high school guidance counselors, the career services office at technical or community colleges, and the associations listed at the end of this article are other helpful resources that will help you learn more about the career of petroleum engineer.

EMPLOYERS

Petroleum engineers are employed by major oil companies, as well as smaller oil companies. They work in oil exploration and production. Some petroleum engineers are employed by consulting companies and equipment suppliers. The federal government is also an employer of engineers. In the United States, oil or natural gas is produced in 42 states, with most sites located in California, Louisiana, Oklahoma, and Texas, plus offshore regions. Many other engineers work in other oil-producing areas such as the Arctic Circle, China's Tarim Basin, and the Middle East. Approximately 16,000 petroleum engineers are employed in the United States.

STARTING OUT

The most common and perhaps the most successful way to obtain a petroleum engineering job is to apply for positions through the career services office at the college you attend. Oil companies often have recruiters who seek potential graduates while they are in their last year of engineering school.

Applicants are also advised to simply check the job sections of major newspapers and apply directly to companies seeking employees. They should also keep informed of the general national employment outlook in this industry by reading trade and association journals, such as the Society of Petroleum Engineers' *Journal of Petroleum Technology* (http://www.spe.org/spe-app/spe/jpt/index.htm).

Engineering internships and co-op programs where students attend classes for a portion of the year and then work in an engineering-related job for the remainder of the year allow students to graduate with valuable work experience sought by employers. Many times these students are employed full time after graduation at the place where they had their internship or co-op job.

As in most engineering professions, entry-level petroleum engineers first work under the supervision of experienced professionals for a number of years. New engineers usually are assigned to a field location where they learn different aspects of field petroleum engineering. Initial responsibilities may include well productivity, reservoir and enhanced recovery studies, production equipment and application design, efficiency analyses, and economic evaluations. Field assignments are followed by other opportunities in regional and headquarters offices.

ADVANCEMENT

After several years working under professional supervision, engineers can begin to move up to higher levels. Workers often formulate a choice of direction during their first years on the job. In the operations division, petroleum engineers can work their way up from the field to district, division, and then operations manager. Some engineers work through various engineering positions from field engineer to staff, then division, and finally chief engineer on a project. Some engineers may advance into top executive management. In any position, however, continued enrollment in educational courses is usually required to keep abreast of technological progress and changes. After about four years of work experience, engineers usually apply for a P.E. license so they can be certified to work on a larger number of projects.

Others get their master's or doctoral degree so they can advance to more prestigious research engineering, university-level teaching, or consulting positions. Also, petroleum engineers may transfer to many other occupations, such as economics, environmental management, and groundwater hydrology. Finally, some entrepreneurial-minded workers become independent operators and owners of their own oil companies.

EARNINGS

Petroleum engineers with a bachelor's degree earned average starting salaries of $61,516 in 2005, according to the National Association of Colleges and Employers. A survey by the Society of Petroleum Engineers reports that its worldwide members earned an average salary of $108,742 in 2006. The survey also reports the following average salaries in 2006 for U.S. petroleum engineers by years of experience: zero to 10 years, $75,168; 16 to 20 years, $111,902; and 26 or more years, $121,201.

Salary rates tend to reflect the economic health of the petroleum industry as a whole. When the price of oil is high, salaries can be expected to grow; low oil prices often result in stagnant wages.

Fringe benefits for petroleum engineers are good. Most employers provide health and accident insurance, sick pay, retirement plans, profit-sharing plans, and paid vacations. Education benefits are also competitive.

WORK ENVIRONMENT

Petroleum engineers work all over the world: the high seas, remote jungles, vast deserts, plains, and mountain ranges. Petroleum engineers who are assigned to remote foreign locations may be separated from their families for long periods or be required to resettle their families when new job assignments arise. Those working overseas may live in company-supplied housing.

Some petroleum engineers, such as drilling engineers, work primarily out in the field at or near drilling sites in all kinds of weather and environments. The work can be dirty and dangerous. Responsibilities such as making reports, conducting studies of data, and analyzing costs are usually tended to in offices either away from the site or in temporary work trailers.

Other engineers work in offices in cities of varying sizes, with only occasional visits to an oil field. Research engineers work in laboratories much of the time, while those who work as professors spend most of their time on campuses. Workers involved in economics, management, consulting, and government service tend to spend their work time exclusively indoors.

OUTLOOK

Employment for petroleum engineers is expected to decline through 2014, according to the U.S. Department of Labor. Despite this prediction, opportunities for petroleum engineers will exist because the number of degrees granted in petroleum engineering is low, leaving more job openings than there are qualified candidates. Additionally, employment opportunities may improve as a result of the federal government's plans to construct new gas refineries, pipelines, and transmission lines, as well as to drill in areas that were previously off-limits to such development.

The challenge for petroleum engineers in the past decade has been to develop technology that lets drilling and production be economically feasible even in the face of low oil prices. For example, engineers had to rethink how they worked in deep water. They used to believe deep wells would collapse if too much oil was pumped out at once. But the high costs of working in deep water plus low oil prices made low volumes uneconomical. So engineers learned how to boost oil flow by slowly increasing the quantities wells pumped by improving valves, pipes, and other equipment used. Engineers have also cut the cost of deep-water oil and gas production in the Gulf of Mexico, predicted to be one of the most significant exploration hot spots in the world for the next decade, by placing wellheads on the ocean floor instead of on above-sea production platforms.

Cost-effective technology that permits new drilling and increases production will continue to be essential in the profitability of the oil industry. Therefore, petroleum engineers will continue to have a vital role to play, even in this age of streamlined operations and company restructurings.

FOR MORE INFORMATION

For information on careers in petroleum geology, contact
American Association of Petroleum Geologists
PO Box 979
Tulsa, OK 74101-0979
Tel: 800-364-2274
http://www.aapg.org

For information on summer programs, contact
American Indian Science and Engineering Society
PO Box 9828
Albuquerque, NM 87119-9828
Tel: 505-765-1052

Email: info@aises.org
http://www.aises.org

For general information on the petroleum industry, contact
American Petroleum Institute
1220 L Street, NW
Washington, DC 20005-4070
Tel: 202-682-8000
http://www.api.org

*For information about JETS programs, products, and engineering
career brochures (all disciplines), contact*
Junior Engineering Technical Society (JETS)
1420 King Street, Suite 405
Alexandria, VA 22314-2750
Tel: 703-548-5387
Email: info@jets.org
http://www.jets.org

*For a petroleum engineering career brochure, a list of petroleum
engineering schools, and scholarship information, contact*
Society of Petroleum Engineers
PO Box 833836
Richardson, TX 75083-3836
Tel: 800-456-6863
Email: spedal@spe.org
http://www.spe.org

*For information on career guidance literature, scholarships, and
mentor programs, contact*
Society of Women Engineers
230 East Ohio Street, Suite 400
Chicago, IL 60611-3265
Tel: 312-596-5223
Email: hq@swe.org
http://www.swe.org

For a Frontiers program brochure and application, contact
Worcester Polytechnic Institute
100 Institute Road
Worcester, MA 01609-2280
Tel: 508-831-5286
Email: frontiers@wpi.edu
http://www.admissions.wpi.edu/Frontiers

Petroleum Technicians

QUICK FACTS

School Subjects
Mathematics
Physics

Personal Skills
Helping/teaching
Technical/scientific

Work Environment
Indoors and outdoors
Primarily multiple locations

Minimum Education Level
High school diploma

Salary Range
$22,020 to $46,160 to
$88,150+

Certification or Licensing
None available

Outlook
More slowly than the average

DOT
010

GOE
02.05.01, 06.03.01

NOC
2212

O*NET-SOC
19-4041.00, 47-5011.00,
47-5012.00, 47-5013.00,
47-5021.01

OVERVIEW

Petroleum technicians work in a wide variety of specialties. Many kinds of *drilling technicians* drill for petroleum from the earth and beneath the ocean. *Loggers* analyze rock cuttings from drilling and measure characteristics of rock layers. Various types of *production technicians* "complete" wells (prepare wells for production), collect petroleum from producing wells, and control production. *Engineering technicians* help improve drilling technology, maximize field production, and provide technical assistance. *Maintenance technicians* keep machinery and equipment running smoothly. There are approximately 11,000 petroleum and geological technicians employed in the United States.

HISTORY

In the 1950s and 1960s, the oil industry was relatively stable. Oil was cheap and much in demand. The international oil market was dominated by the "seven sisters"—Shell, Esso, BP, Gulf, Chevron, Texaco, and Mobil. However, by the end of the 1960s, Middle Eastern countries became more dominant. Many nationalized the major oil companies' operations or negotiated to control oil production. To promote and protect their oil production and revenues gained, Iran, Iraq, Kuwait, Saudi Arabia, and Venezuela formed OPEC (the Organization of Petroleum Exporting Countries). The Arab producers' policies during the Arab/Israeli War of 1973–74 and the Iranian Revolution in 1978 disrupted oil supplies and skyrocketed oil prices, indicating just how powerful OPEC had become.

By the early 1980s, economic recession and energy conservation measures had resulted in lower oil prices. There was—and still is—worldwide surplus production capacity. OPEC, which expanded membership to countries in the Far East and Africa, tried to impose quotas limiting production, with little success. In 1986, prices—which had once again risen—plummeted.

In the 1990s and 2000s, factors such as strong demand from a growing U.S. population, reductions in domestic oil exploration and production, and conflicts in oil-producing countries such as Iraq caused a significant increase in the price of petroleum.

The events of the 1960s through today have significantly altered the nation's attitude toward the price and availability of petroleum products. The federal government and domestic oil companies have come to realize that foreign sources of oil could easily be lost through regional conflicts or international tensions. To address this crisis, the U.S. government has set a goal of increased domestic production.

These developments have fostered great changes in the technology of oil drilling, in the science related to oil exploration, and in the management of existing oil fields. In many old abandoned fields, scientists found that nearly as much oil remained as had originally been produced from them by older methods. New technology is constantly being developed and used to find ways of extracting more of this remaining oil economically from old and new fields alike.

The career of petroleum technician was created to help the industry meet such challenges. Technological changes require scientifically competent technical workers as crewmembers for well drilling and oil field management. Well-trained technicians are essential to the oil industry and will continue to be in the future.

THE JOB

Before petroleum technicians can begin work on an oil reservoir, prospective sites must first be sought by geological exploration teams. These crews perform seismic surveying, in which sound waves are created and their reflection from underground rocks recorded by seismographs, to help locate potential sources of oil. Other team members collect and examine geological data or test geological samples to determine petroleum and mineral content. They may also use surveying and mapping instruments and techniques to help locate and map test holes or the results of seismic tests.

It is the drill bit, however, that ultimately proves whether or not there is oil. Drilling for oil is a highly skilled operation involving many kinds of technicians: *rotary drillers, derrick operators, engine operators*, and *tool pushers*.

In the most common type of drilling, a drill bit with metal or diamond teeth is suspended on a drilling string consisting of 30-foot pipes joined together. The string is added to as the bit goes deeper. The bit is turned either by a rotary mechanism on the drill floor or, increasingly, by a downhole motor. As drilling progresses, the bit gets worn and has to be replaced. The entire drilling string, sometimes weighing more than 100 tons must be hauled to the surface and dismantled section by section, the bit replaced, then the string reassembled and run back down the well. Known as a "round trip," this operation can take the drilling crew most of a 12-hour shift in a deep well. Until recently, drill strings were mostly manually handled; however, mechanized drill rigs that handle pipe automatically have been introduced to improve safety and efficiency.

The driller directs the crew and is responsible for the machinery operation. The driller watches gauges and works throttles and levers to control the hoisting and rotation speed of the drill pipe and the amount of weight on the bit. Special care is needed as the bit nears oil and gas to avoid a "blow-out." Such "gushers" were common in the early days of the oil industry, but today's drilling technicians are trained to prevent them. Drillers also are responsible for recording the type and depth of strata penetrated each day and materials used.

Derrick operators are next in charge of the drilling crew. They work on a platform high up on the derrick and help handle the upper end of the drilling string during placement and removal. They also mix the special drilling "mud" that is pumped down through the pipe to lubricate and cool the bit as well as help control the flow of oil and gas when oil is struck.

Engine operators run engines to supply power for rotary drilling machinery and oversee their maintenance. They may help when the roughnecks pull or add pipe sections.

Tool pushers are in charge of one or more drilling rigs. They oversee erection of the rig, the selection of drill bits, the operation of drilling machinery, and the mixing of drilling mud. They arrange for the delivery of tools, machinery, fuel, water, and other supplies to the drilling site.

One very specialized drilling position is the *oil-well fishing-tool technician*. These technicians analyze conditions at wells where some object, or "fish," has obstructed the borehole. They direct the work of removing the obstacle (lost equipment or broken drill pipes, for example), choosing from a variety of techniques.

During drilling, *mud test technicians*, also called *mud loggers*, use a microscope at a portable laboratory on-site to analyze drill cuttings carried out of the well by the circulating mud for traces of oil. After final depth is reached, technicians called *well loggers* lower measuring devices to the bottom of the well on cable called wireline. Wireline logs examine the electrical, acoustic, and radioactive properties of the rocks and provide information about rock type and porosity, and how much fluid (oil, gas, or water) it contains. These techniques, known as formation evaluation, help the operating company decide whether enough oil exists to warrant continued drilling.

The first well drilled is an exploration well. If oil is discovered, more wells, called appraisal wells, are drilled to establish the limits of the field. Then the field's economic worth and profit are evaluated. If it is judged economically worthwhile to develop the field, some of the appraisal wells may be used as production wells. The production phase of the operation deals with bringing the well fluids to the surface and preparing them for their trip through the pipeline to the refinery.

The first step is to complete the well—that is, to perform whatever operations are needed to start the well fluids flowing to the surface—and is performed by *well-servicing technicians*. These technicians use a variety of well-completion methods, determined by the oil reservoir's characteristics. Typical tasks include setting and cementing pipe (called production casing) so that the oil can come to the surface without leaking into the upper layers of rock. Well-servicing technicians may later perform maintenance work to improve or maintain the production from a formation already producing oil. These technicians bring in smaller rigs similar to drilling rigs for their work.

After the well has been completed, a structure consisting of control valves, pressure gauges, and chokes (called a Christmas tree because of the way its fittings branch out) is assembled at the top of the well to control the flow of oil and gas. Generally, production crews direct operations for several wells.

Well fluids are often a mixture of oil, gas, and water and must be separated and treated before going into the storage tanks. After separation, *treaters* apply heat, chemicals, electricity, or all three to remove contaminants. They also control well flow when the natural pressure is great enough to force oil from the well without pumping.

Pumpers operate, monitor, and maintain production facilities. They visually inspect well equipment to make sure it's functioning properly. They also detect and perform any routine maintenance needs. They adjust pumping cycle time to optimize production and measure the fluid levels in storage tanks, recording the information each day for entry on weekly gauge reports. Pumpers also advise oil haulers or purchasers when a tank is ready for sale.

Gaugers ensure that other company personnel and purchasers comply with the company's oil measurement and sale policy. They spotcheck oil measurements and resolve any discrepancies. They also check pumpers' equipment for accuracy and arrange for the replacement of malfunctioning gauging equipment.

Once a field has been brought into production, good reservoir management is needed to ensure that as much oil as possible is recovered. *Production engineering technicians* work with the production engineers to plan field workovers and well stimulation techniques such as secondary and tertiary recovery (for example, injecting steam, water, or a special recovery fluid) to maximize field production. *Reservoir engineering technicians* provide technical assistance to reservoir engineers. They prepare spreadsheets for analyses required for economic evaluations and forecasts. They also gather production data and maintain well histories and decline curves on both company-operated and outside-operated wells.

The petroleum industry has a need for other kinds of technicians as well, including *geological technicians*, *chemical technicians*, and *civil engineering technicians*.

REQUIREMENTS

All petroleum technician jobs require at least a high school diploma, and a few specialties require at least a bachelor's degree.

High School

If you are interested in this field, you should begin preparing in high school by taking math, algebra, geometry, trigonometry, and calculus classes. Earth science, chemistry, and physics are other useful subjects. High school courses in drafting, mechanics, or auto shop are also valuable preparation, especially for drilling and production technicians. Computer skills are particularly important for engineering technicians, as are typing and English courses.

Postsecondary Training

As mentioned above, postsecondary training is required for only a few petroleum technician positions. For example, a mud test technician must have at least a bachelor's degree in geology. Although postsecondary training is not usually required for drilling, production, or engineering technicians, these workers can gain familiarity with specified basic processes through special education in technical or community colleges. Postsecondary training can also help entry-level workers compete with experienced workers.

Petroleum technology programs, located primarily at schools in the West and Southwest, are helpful both for newcomers to the field and for those trying to upgrade their job skills. An associate's degree in applied science can be earned by completing a series of technical and education courses.

Petroleum technology programs provide training in drilling operations, fluids, and equipment; production methods; formation evaluation along with the basics of core analysis; and well completion methods and petroleum property evaluation, including evaluation of production history data and basic theories and techniques of economic analysis. These programs emphasize practical applications in the laboratory, field trips, and summer employment, as available.

Specialized training programs designed for oil company employees are offered by the suppliers of the special materials, equipment, or services.

Other Requirements

Petroleum technicians must be able to work with accuracy and precision; mistakes can be costly or hazardous to the technician and to others in the workplace. You should also be able to work both independently and as part of a team, display manual dexterity, mathematical aptitude, and be willing to work irregular hours.

Much of the work in the petroleum industry involves physical labor and is potentially dangerous. Field technicians must be strong and healthy, enjoy the outdoors in all weather, and be flexible and adaptable about working conditions and hours. Drilling crews may be away from their home base for several days at a time, while technicians on offshore rigs must be able to deal with a restricted environment for several days at a time. Petroleum technicians must also like working with machinery, scientific equipment and instruments, and computers. In addition, petroleum technicians must have good eyesight and hearing and excellent hand, eye, and body coordination.

Some technicians must operate off-road vehicles to transport people, supplies, and equipment to drilling and production sites. Most of this task is learned on the job after formal training is completed.

Some petroleum technicians require additional safety training, including hazardous materials training and first-aid training. In some cases, special physical examinations and drug testing are required. Testing and examinations generally take place after technicians are hired.

EXPLORING

You may want to investigate petroleum technician occupations further by checking your school or public libraries for books on the petroleum industry. Other resources include trade journals, high school guidance counselors, the career services office at technical or community colleges, and the associations and Web sites listed at the end of this article. If you live near an oil field, you may be able to arrange a tour by contacting the public relations department of oil companies or drilling contractors.

Summer and other temporary jobs on drilling and production crews are excellent ways of finding out about this field. Temporary work can provide you with firsthand knowledge of the basics of oil field operations, equipment maintenance, safety, and other aspects of the work. You may also want to consider entering a two-year training program in petroleum technology to learn about the field.

EMPLOYERS

Although drilling for oil and gas is conducted in 42 states, nearly 75 percent of workers in this field are employed in four states: California, Louisiana, Oklahoma, and Texas. Employers in the crude petroleum and natural gas industry include major oil companies and independent producers. The oil and gas field services industry, which includes drilling contractors, logging companies, and well servicing contractors, is the other major source of employment. Approximately 11,000 petroleum and geological technicians are employed in the United States.

STARTING OUT

You may enter the field of petroleum drilling or production as a laborer or general helper if you have completed high school. From there, you can work your way up to highly skilled technical jobs, responsibilities, and rewards.

Engineering technicians might start out as *engineering* or *production secretaries* and advance to the position of technician after two to five years of on-the-job experience and demonstrated competency in the use of computers.

Other technicians, such as mud test loggers or well loggers, will need a geology degree first. Upon obtaining your degree, you may start out as an assistant to experienced geologists or petroleum engineers.

Generally speaking, industry recruiters from major companies and employers regularly visit the career services offices of schools with petroleum technology programs and hire technicians before they finish their last year of technical school or college.

Because many graduates have little or no experience with well drilling operations, new technicians work primarily as assistants to the leaders of the operations. They may also help with the semiskilled or skilled work in order to become familiar with the skills and techniques needed.

It is not uncommon, however, for employers to hire newly graduated technicians and immediately send them to a specialized training program. These programs are designed for oil company employees and usually are offered by the suppliers of the special materials, equipment, or services. After the training period, technicians may be sent anywhere in the world where the company has exploratory drilling or production operations.

ADVANCEMENT

In oil drilling and production, field advancement comes with experience and on-the-job competency. Although a petroleum technology degree is generally not required, it is clearly helpful in today's competitive climate. On a drilling crew, the usual job progression is as follows: from roughneck or rig builder to derrick operator, rotary driller, to tool pusher, and finally, oil production manager. In production, pumpers and gaugers may later become oil company production foremen or operations foremen; from there, they may proceed to operations management, which oversees an entire district. Managers who begin as technicians gain experience that affords them special skills and judgment.

Self-employment also offers interesting and lucrative opportunities. For example, because many drilling rigs are owned by small, private owners, technicians can become independent owners and operators of drilling rigs. The rewards for successfully operating an independent drill can be very great, especially if the owner discovers new fields and shares in the royalties for production.

Working as a consultant or a technical salesperson can lead to advancement in the petroleum industry. Success is contingent upon an excellent record of field success in oil and gas drilling and production.

In some areas, advancement requires further education. Well loggers who want to analyze logs are required to have at least a bachelor's degree in geology or petroleum engineering, and sometimes they need a master's degree. With additional schooling and a bachelor's degree, an engineering technician can become an engineer. For advanced level engineering, a master's degree is the minimum requirement and a doctorate is typically required. Upper-level researchers also need a doctorate.

During periods of rapid growth in the oil industry, advancement opportunities are plentiful for capable workers. However, downsizing in recent years has made advancement more difficult, and in many cases technicians, geologists, engineers, and others have accepted positions for which they are overqualified.

EARNINGS

Because of their many work situations and conditions, petroleum technicians' salaries vary widely. Salaries also vary according to geographic location, experience, and education. Petroleum and geological technicians had median annual earnings of $46,160 in 2006, according to the U.S. Department of Labor. Salaries ranged from less than $22,020 to $88,150 or more annually.

In general, technicians working in remote areas and under severe weather conditions usually receive higher rates of pay, as do technicians who work at major oil companies and companies with unions.

Fringe benefits are good. Most employers provide health and accident insurance, sick pay, retirement plans, profit-sharing plans, and paid vacations. Education benefits are also competitive.

WORK ENVIRONMENT

Petroleum technicians' workplaces and conditions vary as widely as their duties. They may work on land or offshore, at drilling sites or in laboratories, in offices or refineries.

Field technicians do their work outdoors, day and night, in all kinds of weather. Drilling and production crews work all over the world, often in swamps, deserts, or in the mountains. The work is rugged and physical, and more dangerous than many other kinds of work. Safety is a big concern. Workers are subject to falls and other accidents on rigs, and blowouts can injure or kill workers if well pressure is not controlled.

Drilling crews often move from place to place because work in a particular field may be completed in a few weeks or months. Technicians who work on production wells usually remain in the same location for long periods. Hours are often long for both groups of workers.

Those working on offshore rigs and platforms can experience strong ocean currents, tides, and storms. Living quarters are usually small, like those on a ship, but they are adequate and comfortable. Workers generally live and work on the drilling platform for days at a time and then get several days off away from the rig, returning to shore by helicopter or crewboat.

Engineering technicians generally work indoors in clean, well-lit offices, although some may also spend part of their time in the field. Regular, 40-hour workweeks are the norm, although some may occasionally work irregular hours.

OUTLOOK

Employment of petroleum technicians is expected to grow more slowly than the average for all occupations through 2014, according to the U.S. Department of Labor (DOL). Companies are continuing to restructure and reduce costs in an effort to conserve more money for exploration and drilling abroad and offshore. The implementation of these measures may mean fewer opportunities for petroleum technicians.

Besides looking for new fields, companies are also expending much effort to boost production in existing fields. New cost-effective technology that permits new drilling and increases production will continue to be important in helping the profitability of the oil industry.

Despite its recent difficulties, the oil industry still plays an important role in the economy and employment. Oil and gas will continue to be primary energy sources for many decades. Most job openings will be due to retirements and job transfer. Technicians with specialized training will have the best employment opportunities. The DOL reports that professional, scientific, and technical services firms will increasingly seek the services of petroleum technicians who can act as consultants regarding environmental policy and federal pollution mandates.

FOR MORE INFORMATION

For information on careers in geology and student chapters, contact
American Association of Petroleum Geologists
PO Box 979
Tulsa, OK 74101-0979
Tel: 800-364-2274
http://www.aapg.org

For facts and statistics about the petroleum industry, contact
American Petroleum Institute
1220 L Street, NW
Washington, DC 20005-4070
Tel: 202-682-8000
http://www.api.org

For information about JETS programs, products, and engineering career brochures (all disciplines), contact
Junior Engineering Technical Society (JETS)
1420 King Street, Suite 405
Alexandria, VA 22314-2750

Tel: 703-548-5387
Email: info@jets.org
http://www.jets.org

*For a list of petroleum technology schools and careers in petroleum
engineering, contact*
Society of Petroleum Engineers
PO Box 833836
Richardson, TX 75083-3836
Tel: 800-456-6863
Email: spedal@spe.org
http://www.spe.org

*For a training catalog listing publications, audiovisuals, and short
courses, including correspondence courses, contact*
University of Texas at Austin
Petroleum Extension Service
One University Station, R8100
Austin, TX 78712-1100
Tel: 800-687-4132
http://www.utexas.edu/cee/petex

Pharmacologists

OVERVIEW

Pharmacologists play an important role in medicine and in science by studying the effects of drugs, chemicals, and other substances on humans, animals, and plants. These highly educated scientists conduct research on living tissues and organs to determine how drugs and other chemicals act at the cellular level. Their results help to discover how drugs and other chemicals should be most effectively used. The study of pharmacology is necessary to standardize drug dosages; analyze chemicals, food additives, poisons, insecticides, and other substances; and identify dangerous substances and harmful levels of controlled chemicals.

HISTORY

Pharmacology is not the same as pharmacy. Pharmacology is the science concerned with the interactions between chemicals and biological systems. Pharmacy is the practice of preparation and dispensing of drugs to patients.

Past civilizations, especially the cultures of ancient Greece and China, compiled the earliest written pharmacological knowledge, identifying certain diseases and the recommended "prescriptions" for these ailments. It was not until thousands of years later that organized experiments in pharmacology began. Many credit François Magendie, an early 19th-century French physiologist, with the birth of experimental pharmacology. The research of Magendie and his student, Claude Bernard, on poisons such as strychnine and carbon monoxide, and on the use of curare as a muscle relaxant, helped to establish many of the principles of modern pharmacology. In 1847, a German, Rudolf Bucheim,

QUICK FACTS

School Subjects
Biology
Chemistry
Mathematics

Personal Skills
Communication/ideas
Technical/scientific

Work Environment
Primarily indoors
Primarily one location

Minimum Education Level
Doctorate degree

Salary Range
$71,400 to $114,800 to $147,900+

Certification or Licensing
Voluntary

Outlook
Much faster than the average

DOT
041

GOE
14.02.01

NOC
2121

O*NET-SOC
19-1042.00

started the first institute of pharmacology at the University of Dorpat, establishing the study of pharmacology as a singular discipline. A student of Bucheim, Oswald Schmiedeberg, became a professor of pharmacology and further passed on his knowledge to students from all over the world. One of these students, John Jacob Abel, is credited with bringing experimental pharmacology to the United States.

The medical achievements and discoveries of pharmacologists are numerous. Their work has helped in the development of antibiotics, anesthetics, vaccines, tranquilizers, vitamins, and many other substances in wide medical use today. Pharmacologists have been instrumental, for example, in the use of ether and other anesthetics that have modernized surgical procedures. Their research was used in the development of lifesaving drugs such as penicillin, tetanus and polio vaccines, antimalaria drugs, and countless other compounds. In addition, pharmacologists have helped to develop drugs to treat heart disease, cancer, and psychiatric illnesses.

With the scientific advances of the early 20th century, especially the introduction of antibacterial drugs into medicine, pharmacology gained recognition as a distinct discipline. Spurred by pharmacological research, the Food, Drug, and Cosmetic Act of 1938 was introduced, requiring rigorous studies of drugs before they could be marketed. Regulations continue today through the Food and Drug Administration.

Unlike early pharmacologists who were strictly devoted to developing new drugs, modern pharmacologists perform a much broader range of activities. They test pesticides for harmful reactions, identify poisons and their effects, analyze industrial pollutants, study food preservatives and colorings, and check other substances for their effects on the environment as well as on humans. Their research includes all aspects of modern molecular and cellular biology as well as effects of drugs in animals and humans.

THE JOB

Pharmacologists are highly trained scientists who study the effects drugs and other chemical agents have on humans, animals, and plants. They may create new drugs, test old drugs for new uses, or study the interaction between drugs or other chemical agents and an organism to find out how a disease progresses. Pharmacologists perform research in laboratories using cultured cells, laboratory animals, plants, human tissues, precision electronic instruments, and computers. They try to answer such questions as the following: What is a drug's effect on the cellular system of the tissue or other subject being studied? How is the drug absorbed, distributed, and released from the cells or organism?

Are the cells or organism developing sensitivity to the drug and how is that happening? Pharmacology also involves studying therapeutics and toxicology as they relate to drugs and other chemical agents. Therapeutics refers to the drugs or other agents' action or influence on diseases as well as the diseases' influence on the properties of drugs and other agents. Pharmacologists specializing in drug research, for example, may study the therapeutic effects of medical compounds on specific organs or bodily systems. They identify potentially beneficial and potentially harmful side effects and are then able to predict the drug's usefulness against specific diseases. They also use this information to recommend proper dosages and describe circumstances in which a drug should be administered. Toxicology refers to the toxic effects of drugs used to treat diseases as well as the toxic effects of chemical agents in the environment, agriculture, and industry. Pharmacologists trying to identify if there is a hazardous substance in an environment that is making people ill, for example, are involved in toxicology. They may analyze chemicals to determine if dangerous amounts of lead, mercury, or ammonia are in workplaces, pesticides, food preservatives, or even common household items such as paints, aerosol sprays, and cleaning fluids.

The complex field of pharmacology is divided into several areas in which pharmacologists may choose to specialize. *Neuropharmacologists* focus on drugs relating to the nervous system, including the brain, spinal cord, and nerves. *Cardiovascular pharmacologists* specialize in the effects of drugs relating to the cardiovascular and circulatory systems. *Endocrine pharmacologists* study drug effects on the hormonal balance of the body. *Molecular pharmacologists* study the biochemical and biophysical interactions between drug molecules and cells. *Biochemical and cellular pharmacologists* use biochemistry, cell biology, and physiology to determine how drugs interact and influence the chemical makeup of an organism. *Veterinary pharmacologists* are experts on the use and study of drugs with animals. *Behavioral pharmacologists*, sometimes known as *psychopharmacologists*, specialize in studying drugs that affect such things as behavior patterns, learning processes, and mental illnesses. *Chemotherapy pharmacologists* focus their work on creating drugs that will stop the growth of or kill infectious agents or cancer cells without harming healthy cells. *Clinical pharmacologists* specialize in studying how various drugs and chemical compounds work only in human subjects.

Because this work is so complex, requiring knowledge of many aspects of different sciences, mathematics, and even technology, it is not uncommon for teams of pharmacologists to work together, especially in the development of more complex drugs and compounds capable of treating numerous diseases. Pharmacologists may work for laboratories of pharmaceutical companies or universities. A number also teach at universities or medical schools. Research projects take considerable time to complete. In general, it takes 10 to 15 years for pharmacologists to develop, test, and refine a new drug product before the Food and Drug Administration will approve its use for the public. Throughout this entire process, pharmacologists must pay strict attention to detail and keep accurate documentation.

Dr. Dennis Mungall is the director of clinical pharmacology and anticoagulation services at a family practice residency. His clinical research involves cardiovascular medicine and coagulation disorders. He also works as a teacher, helping physicians-in-training, pharmacy students, and general health care providers understand drug therapies and side effects. "I teach how to streamline care," he says, "so that it's cost-effective and easy for the patients. I teach them how to pick the best therapy that fits the patient's pathology. Drug-drug interactions can cause adverse effects; I teach how to understand these and how to avoid them." Mungall says this work is a science of tailoring drug therapy to the individual patient.

REQUIREMENTS

High School

It takes many years of education to become a pharmacologist, but you can begin to prepare yourself for this work by taking college prep classes while in high school. Naturally, you should take science courses, including biology, chemistry, and physics. If your school offers more advanced science courses, such as molecular biology and organic chemistry, take these as well. You will also need a strong math background, so take four years of mathematics, including algebra, geometry, statistics, trigonometry, pre-calculus, and calculus, if your school offers this. Keep your computer skills up to date by taking computer science classes. Because you will need strong researching, writing, and speaking skills, you should also take four years of English classes.

Postsecondary Training

Your next step after high school is to earn an undergraduate degree. A few universities offer an undergraduate degree in pharmacology. Because of the limited number of schools offering this degree, however, many students choose to get bachelor's degrees in chemistry, biological science, or biochemistry, which are also appropriate. No matter what your major is, your college studies should again focus on sciences (biology, physics, organic and inorganic chemistry) and mathematics (such as differential calculus and integral calculus). Other courses to take include English, computer science, and a foreign language.

After college, you need to complete graduate-level work. To conduct research, teach at a medical school or school of pharmacy, or advance to high level administrative positions, the minimum education you need is a doctorate degree in pharmacology. Many pharmacologists, however, have more than one advanced degree. Some, for example, have a doctorate in another science, such as biochemistry, and a doctorate in pharmacology. Others have medical degrees (M.D.'s) and pharmacology doctorates. Some pharmacologists who specialize in animal pharmacology are also doctors of veterinary medicine (D.V.M.'s). Many courses in pharmacology closely resemble medical school courses, and Ph.D.s in pharmacology are offered at medical schools, schools of pharmacy, and research universities. Certain veterinary schools offer degrees in veterinary pharmacology as well.

The American Society for Pharmacology and Experimental Therapeutics, a professional organization of pharmacologists, provides a list of accredited pharmacology graduate programs as well as other relevant information. (Visit the Training Programs section on its Web site, http://www.aspet.org.) Once you've been accepted to such an institution, the Ph.D. program generally takes between four to six years to complete. Studies involve intensive courses in cellular and molecular biology, physiology, neuroscience, basic and molecular pharmacology, chemotherapy, toxicology, statistics, and research. The major portion of the Ph.D. program requires students to undertake independent and supervised research and successfully complete an original laboratory project. Graduate students must also write a doctoral thesis on their research project.

After receiving their Ph.D., many pharmacologists go on to complete two to four additional years of postdoctoral research training in which they assist a scientist on a second project in order to gain further research skills, experience, and maturity.

Certification or Licensing

Pharmacologists may choose to become certified within a special area of study. The American Board of Clinical Pharmacology, for example, offers certification in clinical and applied pharmacology. Applicants are judged based on training and experience. They must first receive their doctoral degree and complete at least five years of postdoctoral work in clinical pharmacology, among other requirements, before being eligible for the exam.

Other Requirements

"Communication is the most important part of the job," says Dr. Dennis Mungall. "You'll be organizing patients, administrators, people in business, and others—bringing people together for projects."

Mungall also emphasizes creativity. "Being creative," he says, "adds to your ability to be a good researcher, to be a good thinker."

Pharmacologists must be creative, curious, and flexible in order to entertain new ideas or investigative strategies. They need to be patient and willing to work long hours in order to master research that does not provide quick or easy answers. They must also be able to work alone or with similarly dedicated and driven colleagues to the conclusion of a project.

EXPLORING

The best way to learn about pharmacology is to interview professionals in the career. Your high school counselor or science teacher may be able to arrange an interview with a qualified pharmacologist or even help plan a tour of a pharmacological facility.

Contact professional organizations for information about this career. The American Society for Pharmacology and Experimental Therapeutics provides information on the field of pharmacology, including educational programs and academic institutions, the various subspecialties of pharmacology, and laboratories, drug companies, and other branches of the profession that employ pharmacologists.

Medical and other laboratories frequently employ part-time personnel to assist with various tasks. Information regarding summer or part-time opportunities can be obtained by contacting work-study or student research programs and student placement services. But you need to keep in mind that these positions can be hard to come by because you may be competing with pharmacological graduate students for jobs. If you are unable to get one of these positions, consider getting any type of work or experience that will give you the opportunity to be in a laboratory or medical setting. For example, you may be able to volunteer at a local hospital's pharmacy or find part-time work at a doctor's office. While you may be filing papers and updating computer records, you will also be learning about various drugs and what they do.

EMPLOYERS

Pharmacologists are employed as faculty in medical, dental, veterinary, or pharmacy schools, and as researchers in large hospitals, medical centers, or research institutes. They also work for government agencies involved in research such as the National Institutes of Health, the Environmental Protection Agency, and the Food and Drug Administration.

Pharmacology in the 21st Century

The American Society for Pharmacology and Experimental Therapeutics predicts that pharmacologists will focus on the following issues in the 21st century:

- adverse drug reactions
- anticancer and antiviral agents
- behavioral pharmacology
- cancer chemotherapy
- cellular pharmacology
- combinatorial pharmacology
- developmental pharmacology
- environmental pharmacology
- gastrointestinal pharmacology
- gene therapies
- geriatric pharmacology
- immunopharmacology
- pharmacogenetics
- pulmonary pharmacology
- recombinant-DNA-derived drugs
- traditional and herbal medicines

Source: *Explore Pharmacology: Graduate Studies in Pharmacology,* American Society for Pharmacology and Experimental Therapeutics

STARTING OUT

Drug companies, research organizations, medical, dental, and pharmacy schools and universities, and federal and state governments often recruit pharmacologists while they are in the process of earning their doctorates. By the second year of their doctoral program, most pharmacologists have chosen a subspecialty and seek out employers representing their chosen area.

If you have not taken a job with an organization recruiting on your campus, you should be able to consult your school's career services office for job leads. If there are research institutes or pharmaceutical and chemical companies of interest to you, you can send resumes directly to them. Additionally, pharmacological journals often list job openings, and professional organizations usually provide employment services or news.

ADVANCEMENT

Most beginning pharmacologists start out in academics at the assistant professor level or work in laboratories, assisting advanced pharmacologists in research. Beginning pharmacologists work to improve their laboratory procedures, learn how to work with the Food and Drug Administration and various other government agencies, and gain experience testing drugs and other substances on both animal and human subjects. In research institutes, private industry, and academic laboratories, advancement in the field of pharmacology usually means moving into a supervising position, overseeing other scientists in a laboratory setting and heading up major research projects. Pharmacologists who work as teachers advance by serving as department heads, supervising research laboratories at universities, presenting public papers, and speaking at major conferences.

Pharmacologists often view their advancements in terms of successful research projects. Dr. Dennis Mungall is looking forward to branching out into other areas to combine his interests in pharmacology, writing, and the Internet. "I have a grant from the American Heart Association to do just that," he says, "using the Internet to improve health care communication with patients."

EARNINGS

A 2006 survey by the American Association of Pharmaceutical Scientists places average base salaries (excluding bonuses) for pharmacologists at $114,800 a year. Salaries ranged from less than $85,000 to $140,000 or more. Pharmaceutical scientists working in industry earned the highest salaries, $109,000 a year. Those in academia averaged $90,100, while those in government earned $100,500. The survey also compared salaries by education level and work experience. Pharmacologists with a master's degree and zero to five years of experience earned annual mean salaries of $71,400; with 10 to 19 years, $105,500; and 30 or more years, $130,400. Pharmacologists with a Ph.D. and zero to five years of experience earned annual mean salaries of $86,400; with 10 to 19 years, $134,000; and 30 or more years, $147,900. Bonuses, especially for those in industry, can increase yearly earnings considerably.

Benefits generally include health and dental insurance and paid vacation and sick days.

WORK ENVIRONMENT

Pharmacologists work in academic settings or laboratories and generally work 40 hours a week, though they may sometimes be required to work extra hours to monitor experiments that need special attention. Most laboratories associated with academic or major research institutions are clean, well-lit, pleasant workplaces equipped with the sophisticated instruments necessary for modern research. Because pharmacologists perform such a vital role with respect to drug and chemical research, their laboratories tend to be fairly up-to-date.

Pharmacologists often work on projects that require years of effort and may for months show seemingly little progress. Pharmacologists must be able to deal with other professionals during what can be frustrating times as research and experiments do not go as planned. They must also be able to deal with the potential stresses associated with working in close quarters with others, sharing laboratory space or other resources.

In some cases, pharmacologists are called upon to work with forensic biologists, coroners, or others involved in determining causes of death under specific circumstances. They may also be asked to travel to other research institutions to share their findings.

OUTLOOK

Although the U.S. Department of Labor does not provide information on pharmacologists, it does recognize the related position of medical scientist (scientists involved with researching the causes of disease and finding treatments). The department predicts that employment for medical scientists will grow much faster than the average for all occupations through 2014, although competition for jobs will be extremely keen. This is because research work is dependent on funding, typically from government sources. In recent years government cutbacks have limited the amount of funding available and, thus, limited research and work opportunities. Pharmacologists, who are also dependent on funding for research projects, are likely to face this same stiff competition for money and jobs. So while the employment outlook overall is good, only those with the most advanced and updated education will have the best prospects in future expanding and specialized job markets.

Areas in which growth is expected include health care, education, and research. Expanding health care needs and services should result in employment opportunities for pharmacologists in drug companies, hospitals, and medical and pharmacy schools. Pharmacological research done by government agencies will also continue.

Teaching opportunities should be plentiful as schools, universities, and medical centers will need qualified pharmacologists to train future students.

The growing elderly population will require pharmacologists to conduct more drug research and development. Pharmacology is also crucial in the development of drugs to battle existing diseases and medical conditions such as AIDS, muscular dystrophy, and cancer, and to facilitate the success of organ transplants.

Further study into drug addiction, gene therapy, and the effect of chemical substances on the environment, including their relationship to cancer and birth defects, will also provide research opportunities for qualified pharmacologists. The increasing interest in more non-traditional medical treatments will also open doors to pharmacologists in such subspecialties as herbal pharmacology, which focuses on the medicinal values of plants.

FOR MORE INFORMATION

To learn more about pharmacology and read news of interest to those in the field, visit the AAPS Web site.

American Association of Pharmaceutical Scientists (AAPS)
2107 Wilson Boulevard, Suite 700
Arlington, VA 22201-3042
Tel: 703-243-2800
http://www.aapspharmaceutica.com

For information on certification, contact

American Board of Clinical Pharmacology
PO Box 40278
San Antonio, TX 78229-1278
Tel: 210-567-8505
http://www.abcp.net

For information on undergraduate and graduate programs in pharmacology, the online publications Explore Pharmacology *and* Medicine by Design, *and a career center for students, visit the ASPET Web site.*

American Society for Pharmacology and Experimental Therapeutics (ASPET)
9650 Rockville Pike
Bethesda, MD 20814-3995
Tel: 301-634-7060
Email: info@aspet.org
http://www.aspet.org

Plastics Engineers

OVERVIEW

Plastics engineers engage in the manufacture, fabrication, and end use of existing materials, as well as in the development of new materials, processes, and equipment. The term, plastics engineering, encompasses a wide variety of applications and manufacturing processes. Depending on the processes involved, plastics engineers develop everything from the initial part design to the processes and automation required to produce and finish the production parts.

HISTORY

Thermoplastics, plastics that soften with heat and harden when cooled, were discovered in France in 1828. In the United States in 1869, a printer, John Wesley Hyatt, created celluloid in the process of attempting to create an alternate material to supplement ivory in billiard balls. His invention, patented in 1872, brought about a revolution in production and manufacturing. By 1892, over 2,500 articles were being produced from celluloid. Among these inventions were frames for eyeglasses, false teeth, the first movie film, and, of course, billiard balls. Celluloid did have its drawbacks. It could not be molded and it was highly flammable.

It was not until 1909 that the Belgian-American chemist Leo H. Baekeland produced the first synthetic plastic. This product replaced natural rubber in electrical insulation and was used for phone handsets and automobile distributor caps and rotors, and is still used today. Other plastics materials have been developed steadily. The greatest variety of materials and applications,

QUICK FACTS

School Subjects
Chemistry
Computer science

Personal Skills
Mechanical/manipulative
Technical/scientific

Work Environment
Primarily indoors
Primarily one location

Minimum Education Level
Bachelor's degree

Salary Range
$46,120 to $73,990 to $112,140+

Certification or Licensing
Required for certain positions (licensing)

Outlook
About as fast as the average

DOT
019

GOE
02.07.02

NOC
2134

O*NET-SOC
17-2131.00

however, came during World War II, when the war effort brought about a need for changes in clothing, consumer goods, transportation, and military equipment.

Today, plastics manufacturing is a major industry whose products play a vital role in many other industries and activities around the world. It is difficult to find an area of our lives where plastic does not play some role. For example, plastics engineers assisting those in the medical field may help to further develop artificial hearts, replacement limbs, artificial skin, implantable eye lenses, and specially designed equipment that will aid surgeons and other health professionals in the operating room.

THE JOB

Plastics engineers perform a wide variety of duties depending on the type of company they work for and the products it produces. Plastics engineers, for example, may develop ways to produce clear, durable plastics to replace glass in areas where glass cannot be used. Others design and manufacture lightweight parts for aircraft and automobiles, or create new plastics to replace metallic or wood parts that have come to be too expensive or hard to obtain. Others may be employed to formulate less-expensive, fire-resistant plastics for use in the construction of houses, offices, and factories. Plastics engineers may also develop new types of biodegradable molecules that are friendly to the environment, reducing pollution and increasing recyclability.

Plastics engineers perform a variety of duties. Some of their specific job titles and duties include: *application engineers*, who develop new processes and materials in order to create a better finished product; *process engineers*, who oversee the production of reliable, high quality, standard materials; and *research specialists*, who use the basic building blocks of matter to discover and create new materials.

In the course of their day, plastics engineers must solve a wide variety of internal production problems. Duties include making sure the process is consistent to ensure creation of accurate and precise parts and making sure parts are handled and packaged efficiently, properly, and cheaply. Each part is unique in this respect.

Computers are increasingly being used to assist in the production process. Plastics engineers use computers to calculate part weight and cycle times; for monitoring the process on each molding press; for designing parts and molds on a computer-aided design system; for tracking processes and the labor in the mold shop; and to transfer engineering files over the Internet.

Plastics engineers also help customers solve problems that may emerge in part design—finding ways to make a part more moldable or to address possible failures or inconsistencies in the final design. Factors that may make a part difficult to mold include: thin walls, functional or cosmetic factors, sections that are improperly designed that will not allow the part to be processed efficiently, or inappropriate material selection which results in an improperly created part.

Plastics engineers also coordinate mold-building schedules and activities with tool vendors. Mold-building schedules consist of the various phases of constructing a mold, from the development of the tool and buying of materials (and facilitating their timely delivery), to estimating the roughing and finishing operations. Molds differ depending on the size of the tool or product, the complexity of the work orders, and the materials required to build the mold.

Most important, plastics engineers must take an application that is difficult to produce and make it (in the short period of time allowed) profitable to their company, while still satisfying the needs of the customer.

REQUIREMENTS

High School
If you are interested in a career as a plastics engineer, follow your school's college prep program by taking classes in English, government, foreign language, and history. You should take additional classes in mathematics and the sciences, particularly chemistry and physics. Computer classes are also important. You should also take vo-tech, drafting, and other classes that involve you directly with design and manufacturing.

Postsecondary Training
The level of education required beyond high school for plastics engineers varies greatly depending on the types of plastics processes involved. Most plastics companies do not require a bachelor's degree in plastics engineering. Companies that design proprietary parts usually require a bachelor's or advanced degree in mechanical engineering. The field of plastics engineering, overall, is still a field where people with the proper experience are scarce—experience is a key factor in qualifying a person for an engineering position.

To pursue an associate's or bachelor's degree in plastics engineering, you should contact the Society of the Plastics Industry (SPI) for information about two- and four-year programs. Plastics programs are sometimes listed under polymer science, polymer engineering, materials science, and materials engineering. Certain branches of the military also provide training in plastics engineering.

Students who plan to enter the military should investigate branches of service that offer training in plastics. The U.S. Air Force, Navy, Coast Guard, and Army publish procurement specifications, operate repair facilities, and carry on their own research and development.

Certification or Licensing

Engineers whose work may affect the life, health, or safety of the public must be registered according to regulations in all 50 states and the District of Columbia. Applicants for registration must have received a degree from an accredited engineering program and have four years of experience. They must also pass a written examination.

Other Requirements

Plastics engineers need to have good mechanical aptitude in order to develop the plastics parts and the tooling necessary to develop these parts. You must have thorough knowledge of the properties of plastic and of the processes that occur. There are thousands of different materials that you may encounter in the course of your workday. You also must be imaginative and creative in order to be able to solve any problems that might arise from new applications or in the transition/transformation of a mechanical metal part to that of a plastic one.

EXPLORING

If you are a high school student, you may seek to join JETS (Junior Engineering Technical Society), an organization that provides organized engineering-related activities. Through group activities you can gain practice in problem solving, scientific reasoning, and actual real life experience with the real world of engineering.

A high school counselor, science, or shop teacher may be able to arrange a presentation or question-and-answer session with a plastics engineer, or even a tour of a local plastics manufacturer. During these tours, you can observe working conditions and discuss employment possibilities with engineers and their managers. There are also student chapters of SPI and the Society of Plastics Engineers (SPE), which provide opportunities to gain valuable experience and contacts with similarly interested people.

Your high school counselor may also arrange visits to community colleges, vocational-technical schools, and universities that offer technical programs.

You may also be able to find a summer job at a plastics-processing plant to learn the basics and experience the varied areas involved with producing plastics parts.

EMPLOYERS

Major plastics employers in the United States include DuPont, General Motors, and Owens Corning. Some of the top thermoforming companies are in Illinois: Pactiv Corporation, Solo Cup Company, and Ivex Packaging LLC are a few of them. Michigan has some of the top injection molding companies, including Lear Corporation and Venture Industries Corporation. But large plastics companies are located all across the country. According to SPI, the top plastics industry states ranked by employment are California, Ohio, Michigan, Texas, and Illinois.

STARTING OUT

To get a job as a plastics engineer, you will need considerable experience in the plastics industry or a college degree. A variety of starting points exist within the industry. Experienced plastics setup and process technicians can use their skills to advance to engineering responsibilities. Many plastics engineers start out as tool and die makers or moldmakers before they move into engineering positions.

For those who receive their plastics knowledge through advanced education, jobs can be obtained through the career services programs of their universities and technical schools. Also, many major companies recruit plastics engineers on college campuses. The SPE Web site features a database of job openings.

Student chapters of the SPE maintain close ties with the parent organization. Student members receive newsletters and technical journals, and they attend professional seminars. These contacts are invaluable when seeking employment.

ADVANCEMENT

The advanced training, expertise, and knowledge of experienced plastics engineers allows them the luxury of migrating to almost any position within the plastics industry. Engineers may also advance to supervisory or management positions, for example, becoming director of engineering for their entire plant or division. Further advancement may come in the form of employment at larger companies. Experienced plastics engineers, as a result of their expertise in materials and matching products to applications, are good candidates for sales and marketing jobs. They may also train the engineers

Did You Know?

Plastics play a key role in protecting durable and perishable goods during shipping, handling, and merchandising. In fact, the American Chemistry Council reports that "400 percent more material by weight would be needed to make packaging if there were no plastics, while the volume of packaging would more than double." Six resins (a solid or semi-solid organic product with no definite melting point) account for almost all of the plastics used in packaging. These include:

- **PET (polyethylene terephthalate)**, which is used in soft drink bottles
- **HDPE (high density polyethylene)**, which is used in juice, milk, and water containers, as well as in containers for household detergents and chemicals
- **PVC (polyvinyl chloride)**, which is used to make packaging for fresh meats
- **LDPE (low density polyethylene)**, which is used to make bottles that must be flexible, as well as create grocery and garbage bags and coating for milk cartons
- **PP (polypropylene)**, which is used for bottle/container caps and lids, for containers that house products that are hot-filled with products (such as ketchup) during the manufacturing process, and for products (such as yogurt) that require incubation during the manufacturing process
- **PS (polystyrene)**, which is used for products such as egg cartons, meat trays, coffee cups, as well as material that protects and packages appliances, electronics, and other delicate goods

Source: American Chemistry Council

of tomorrow by becoming teachers at technical schools or colleges or by writing for a technical trade journal.

EARNINGS

The median annual salary for materials engineers (the category under which the U.S. Department of Labor classifies plastics engineers) was $73,990 in 2006. Salaries ranged from less than $46,120 to $112,140 or more annually.

Benefits for plastics engineers usually include paid vacations and sick days, pension plans, and health and dental insurance. Depending on the size of the company, engineers may be offered production bonuses, stock options, and paid continuing education.

WORK ENVIRONMENT

Plastics engineers are constantly busy as they deal with people at all levels and phases of the manufacturing process. Dress codes may be formal since plastics engineers interact with customers frequently during the course of a day. Engineers may be required to work more than a standard eight-hour day and also some Saturdays when a specific project is on a deadline. Plastics engineers may work directly with design materials in a laboratory or sit at a computer in an office. They may spend some hours working alone, as well as some hours working as part of a team. They may only be involved in certain aspects of a project, or they may work on a project from the original design to final testing of a product.

OUTLOOK

The plastics industry is suffering from the effects of a slowing economy and higher production costs, but most industries are less likely to lay off plastics engineers than other types of workers. More industries are incorporating plastics into their product lines, which will create more opportunities for qualified plastics engineers. As more plastics products are substituted for glass, paper, and metal products and parts, plastics engineers will be needed to oversee design and production processes. Plastics engineers will increasingly be required to develop environmentally friendly products and processes, and play a role in developing easily recyclable products for certain industries. Many openings will come as a result of experienced engineers who advance to sales, management, or other related occupations within the plastics industry. Those with the most advanced skills and experience, as always, will enjoy the best future career outlook. The U.S. Department of Labor predicts job growth for materials engineers, which includes plastics engineers, to be about as fast as the average for all occupations through 2014.

FOR MORE INFORMATION

The Plastics Division of the American Chemistry Council offers a great deal of information about the plastics industry, and maintains an informative Web site.
American Chemistry Council
Plastics Division
1300 Wilson Boulevard
Arlington VA 22209-2323
Tel: 800-243-5790
http://www.americanchemistry.com/plastics

For information on membership and programs, contact
Junior Engineering Technical Society
1420 King Street, Suite 405
Alexandria, VA 22314-2750
Tel: 703-548-5387
Email: info@jets.org
http://www.jets.org

For information about scholarships, seminars, and training, contact
Plastics Institute of America
University of Massachusetts–Lowell Campus
Wannalancit Center
600 Suffolk Street, CVIP, 2nd Floor South
Lowell, MA 01854-3643
Tel: 978-934-3130
Email: contactus@plasticsinstitute.org
http://www.plasticsinstitute.org

For information on obtaining a copy of Plastics Engineering *and information on college scholarships, contact*
Society of Plastics Engineers
14 Fairfield Drive
PO Box 403
Brookfield, CT 06804-0403
Tel: 203-775-0471
Email: info@4spe.org
http://www.4spe.org

For information on careers, college programs, and certification, contact
Society of the Plastics Industry
1667 K Street, NW, Suite 1000
Washington, DC 20006-1620
Tel: 202-974-5200
http://www.socplas.org

For information on career guidance literature, scholarships, and mentor programs, contact
Society of Women Engineers
230 East Ohio Street, Suite 400
Chicago, IL 60611-3265
Tel: 312-596-5223
Email: hq@swe.org
http://www.swe.org

Quality Control Engineers and Technicians

OVERVIEW

Quality control engineers plan and direct procedures and activities that will ensure the quality of materials and goods. They select the best techniques for a specific process or method, determine the level of quality needed, and take the necessary action to maintain or improve quality performance. *Quality control technicians* assist quality control engineers in devising quality control procedures and methods, implement quality control techniques, test and inspect products during different phases of production, and compile and evaluate statistical data to monitor quality levels.

HISTORY

Quality control technology is an outgrowth of the industrial revolution, which began in England in the 18th century. Each person involved in the manufacturing process was responsible for a particular part of the process. The worker's responsibility was further specialized by the introduction of manufacturing with interchangeable parts in the late 18th and early 19th centuries. In a manufacturing process using this technique, a worker concentrated on making just one component, while other workers concentrated on creating other components. Such specialization led to increased production efficiency, especially as manufacturing processes became mechanized during the early part of the 20th century. It also meant, however, that no one worker was responsible for the overall quality of the product. This led to the need for another kind of specialized production worker whose primary responsibility was not one aspect of the product but rather its overall quality.

This responsibility initially belonged to the mechanical engineers and technicians who developed the manufacturing systems, equipment, and procedures. After World War II, however, a new field emerged that was dedicated solely to quality control. Along with specially trained persons to test and inspect products coming off assembly lines, new instruments, equipment, and techniques were developed to measure and monitor specified standards.

At first, quality control engineers and technicians were primarily responsible for random checks of products to ensure they met all specifications. This usually entailed testing and inspecting either finished products or products at various stages of production.

During the 1980s, a renewed emphasis on quality spread across the United States. Faced with increased global competition, especially from Japanese manufacturers, many U.S. companies sought to improve quality and productivity. Quality improvement concepts such as Total Quality Management, Six Sigma, continuous improvement, quality circles, and zero defects gained popularity and changed the way in which companies viewed quality and quality control practices. A new philosophy emerged, emphasizing quality as the concern of all individuals involved in producing goods and directing that quality be monitored at all stages of manufacturing, not just at the end of production or at random stages of manufacturing.

Today, most companies focus on improving quality during all stages of production, with an emphasis on preventing defects rather than merely identifying defective parts. There is an increased use of sophisticated automated equipment that can test and inspect products as they are manufactured. Automated equipment includes cameras, X rays, lasers, scanners, metal detectors, video inspection systems, electronic sensors, and machine vision systems that can detect the slightest flaw or variance from accepted tolerances. Many companies use statistical process control to record levels of quality and determine the best manufacturing and quality procedures. Quality control engineers and technicians work with employees from all departments of a company to train them in the best quality methods and to seek improvements to manufacturing processes to further improve quality levels.

Chemistry students in a lab perform an experiment that determines the weight of a product of a chemical reaction. *(Corbis)*

Many companies today are seeking to conform to international standards for quality, such as ISO 9000 and ISO 14000, in order to compete with foreign companies and to sell products to companies and individuals around the world. These standards are based on concepts of quality of industrial goods and services and involve documenting quality methods and procedures.

THE JOB

Quality control engineers are responsible for developing, implementing, and directing processes and practices that result in a desired level of quality for materials and goods. They identify standards to measure the quality of a part or product, analyze factors that affect quality, and determine the best practices to ensure quality.

Quality control engineers set up procedures to monitor and control quality, devise methods to improve quality, and analyze quality control methods for effectiveness, productivity, and cost factors.

They are involved in all aspects of quality during a product's life cycle. Not only do they focus on ensuring quality during production operations, they are also involved in product design and evaluation. Quality control engineers may be specialists who work with engineers and industrial designers during the design phase of a product, or they may work with sales and marketing professionals to evaluate reports from consumers on how well a product is performing (for example, new plastic packaging that has been developed to extend the shelf life of fresh meat). Quality control engineers are responsible for ensuring that all incoming materials used in a finished product meet required standards and that all instruments and automated equipment used to test and monitor parts during production perform properly. They supervise and direct workers involved in assuring quality, including quality control technicians, inspectors, and related production personnel.

Quality control technicians work with quality control engineers in designing, implementing, and maintaining quality systems. They test and inspect materials and products during all phases of production in order to ensure that they meet specified levels of quality. They may test random samples of products or monitor production workers and automated equipment that inspect products during manufacturing. Using engineering blueprints, drawings, and specifications, they measure and inspect parts for dimensions, performance, and mechanical, electrical, and chemical properties. They establish tolerances, or acceptable deviations from engineering specifications, and they direct manufacturing personnel in identifying rejects and items that need to be reworked. They monitor production processes to ensure that machinery and equipment are working properly and are set to established specifications.

Quality control technicians also record and evaluate test data. Using statistical quality control procedures, technicians prepare charts and write summaries about how well a product conforms to existing standards. Most importantly, they offer suggestions to quality control engineers on how to modify existing quality standards and manufacturing procedures. This helps to achieve the optimum product quality from existing or proposed new equipment.

Quality control technicians may specialize in any of the following areas: product design, incoming materials, process control, product evaluation, inventory control, product reliability, research and development, and administrative applications. Nearly all industries, including the chemical industry, employ quality control technicians.

REQUIREMENTS

High School

To prepare for this career, you should take high school classes in mathematics (including algebra, geometry, and statistics), physical sciences, physics, and chemistry. You should also take shop, mechanical drawing, and computer courses. In addition, you should take English courses that develop your reading skills, your ability to write well-organized reports with a logical development of ideas, and your ability to speak comfortably and effectively in front of a group.

Postsecondary Training

Quality control engineers generally have a bachelor's degree in engineering. Many quality control engineers receive degrees in industrial or manufacturing engineering. Some receive degrees in metallurgical, mechanical, electrical, chemical engineering, or business administration, depending on where they plan to work. College engineering programs vary based on the type of engineering program. Most programs take four to five years to complete and include courses in mathematics, physics, and chemistry. Other useful courses include statistics, logistics, business management, and technical writing.

Educational requirements for quality control technicians vary by industry. Most employers of quality control technicians prefer to hire applicants who have received some specialized training. A small number of positions for technicians require a bachelor of arts or science degree. In most cases, though, completion of a two-year technical program is sufficient. Students enrolled in such a program at a community college or technical school take courses in the physical sciences, mathematics, materials control, materials testing, and engineering-related subjects.

Certification or Licensing

Although there are no licensing or certification requirements designed specifically for quality control engineers or technicians, some need to meet special requirements that apply only within the industry employing them. Many quality control engineers and technicians pursue voluntary certification from professional organizations to indicate that they have achieved a certain level of expertise. The American Society for Quality, for example, offers certification at a number of levels including quality engineer certification, quality process analyst, and quality technician certification. Requirements include having a certain amount of work experience, having proof of professionalism (such as being a licensed professional engineer), and passing a written examination. Many employers value this certification and take it into consideration when making new hires or giving promotions.

Other Requirements

Quality control engineers need scientific and mathematical aptitudes, strong interpersonal skills, and leadership abilities. Good judgment is also needed, as quality control engineers must weigh all the factors influencing quality and determine procedures that incorporate price, performance, and cost factors.

Quality control technicians should do well in mathematics, science, and other technical subjects and should feel comfortable using the language and symbols of mathematics and science. They should have good eyesight and good manual skills, including the ability to use hand tools. They should be able to follow technical instructions and make sound judgments about technical matters. They should have orderly minds and be able to maintain records, conduct inventories, and estimate quantities.

EXPLORING

Quality control engineers and technicians work with scientific instruments; therefore, you should take academic or industrial arts courses that introduce you to different kinds of scientific or technical equipment. You should also take electrical and machine shop courses, mechanical drawing courses, and chemistry courses with lab sections. Joining a radio, computer, or science club is also a good way to gain experience and to engage in team-building and problem-solving activities. Active participation in clubs is a good way to learn skills that will benefit you when working with other professionals in manufacturing and industrial settings. To find out more about engineering in general, join the Junior Engineering Technical Society (JETS), which will give you the opportunity to test your skills and meet professionals and others interested in engineering, math, and science. (Visit the JETS Web site at http://www.jets.org.)

You should keep in mind that quality control activities and quality control professionals are often directly involved with manufacturing processes. If it is at all possible, try to get a part-time or summer job in a manufacturing setting, even if you are not specifically in the quality control area. Although your work may mean doing menial tasks, it will give you firsthand experience in the environment and demonstrate the depth of your interest to future employers.

EMPLOYERS

There are approximately 160,000 industrial production managers (a group that includes quality control engineers) and 69,000 industrial engineering technicians working in the United States. The majority of quality control engineers and technicians are employed in the manufacturing sector of the economy. Because engineers and technicians work in all areas of industry, their employers vary widely in size, product, location, and prestige.

STARTING OUT

Students enrolled in two-year technical schools may learn of openings for quality control technicians through their schools' career services office. Recruiters often visit these schools and interview graduating students for technical positions. Quality control engineers also may learn of job openings through their schools' career services office, recruiters, and job fairs. In many cases, employers prefer to hire engineers who have some work experience in their particular industry. For this reason, applicants who have had summer or part-time employment or participated in a work-study or internship program have greater job opportunities.

Students may also learn about openings through help wanted ads or by using the services of state and private employment services. They also may apply directly to companies that employ quality control engineers and technicians. Students can identify and research such companies by using job resource guides and other reference materials available at most public libraries.

ADVANCEMENT

Quality control technicians usually begin their work under the direct and constant supervision of an experienced technician or engineer. As they gain experience or additional education, they are given assignments with greater responsibilities. They can also become quality control engineers with additional education. Promotion usually depends on additional training as well as job performance. Technicians who obtain additional training have greater chances for advancement opportunities.

Quality control engineers may have limited opportunities to advance within their companies. However, because quality control engineers work in all areas of industry, they have the opportunity to change jobs or companies to pursue more challenging or higher paying positions. Quality control engineers who work in companies with large staffs of quality personnel can become quality control directors or advance to operations management positions.

EARNINGS

Earnings vary according to the type of work, the industry, and the geographical location. Quality control engineers earn salaries comparable to other engineers. According to the U.S. Department of Labor, the median yearly income for industrial production managers was $77,670 in 2006. The lowest paid 10 percent earned less than $47,230, and the highest paid 10 percent made more than $130,680.

The average annual salary for industrial engineering technicians was $46,810 in 2006. Most beginning quality control technicians who are graduates of two-year technical programs earn salaries ranging from $17,000 to $21,000 a year. Experienced technicians with two-year degrees earn salaries that range from $21,000 to $50,000 a year; some senior technicians with special skills or experience may earn much more.

Most companies offer benefits that include paid vacations, paid holidays, and health insurance. Actual benefits depend on the company but may also include pension plans, profit sharing, 401(k) plans, and tuition assistance programs.

WORK ENVIRONMENT

Quality control engineers and technicians work in a variety of settings, and their conditions of work vary accordingly. Most work in manufacturing plants, though the type of industry determines the actual environment. For example, quality control engineers in the metals industry usually work in foundries or iron and steel plants. Conditions there are hot, dirty, and noisy. Other factories, such as for the electronics or pharmaceutical industries, are generally quiet and clean. Most engineers and technicians have offices separate from the production floor, but they still need to spend a fair amount of time there. Engineers and technicians involved with testing and product analysis work in comfortable surroundings, such as a laboratory or workshop. Even in these settings, however, they may be exposed to unpleasant fumes and toxic chemicals. In general, quality control engineers and technicians work inside and are expected to do some light lifting and carrying (usually not more than 20 pounds). Because many manufacturing plants operate 24 hours a day, some quality control technicians may need to work second or third shifts.

As with most engineering and technical positions, the work can be both challenging and routine. Engineers and technicians can expect to find some tasks repetitious and tedious. In most cases, though, the work provides variety and satisfaction from using highly developed skills and technical expertise.

OUTLOOK

The employment outlook for quality control engineers and technicians depends, to some degree, on general economic conditions. The U.S. Department of Labor projects slower than average growth through 2014 for the field of industrial production management, which includes quality control engineers and technicians. This is a result of increased productivity as a result of better technology, in addition to a greater reliance on manufacturing workers to constantly monitor the quality of their own work. However, the roles of the quality control engineer and technician are vital to production and cannot be eliminated. Thus, there will still be new jobs to replace people retiring from or otherwise leaving this field.

Many companies are making vigorous efforts to make their manufacturing processes more efficient, lower costs, and improve productivity and quality. Opportunities for quality control engineers and technicians should be good in the food and beverage industries, pharmaceutical firms, electronics companies, and chemical companies. Quality control engineers and technicians also may find employment in industries using robotics equipment or in the aerospace, biomedical, bioengineering, environmental controls, and transportation industries. Lowered rates of manufacturing in the automotive and defense industries will decrease the number of quality control personnel needed for these areas. Declines in employment in some industries may occur because of the increased use of automated equipment that tests and inspects parts during production operations.

FOR MORE INFORMATION

For information on certification and student chapters, contact
American Society for Quality
PO Box 3005
Milwaukee, WI 53201-3005
Tel: 800-248-1946
Email: help@asq.org
http://www.asq.org

ASTM International offers seminars and other training programs for those involved in testing materials and quality assurance. Visit its Web site to read articles from its magazine Standardization News.

ASTM International
100 Barr Harbor Drive
PO Box C700
West Conshohocken, PA 19428-2959
Tel: 610-832-9585
http://www.astm.org

For information on membership and programs, contact
Junior Engineering Technical Society
1420 King Street, Suite 405
Alexandria, VA 22314-2750
Tel: 703-548-5387
Email: info@jets.org
http://www.jets.org

For information on career guidance literature, scholarships, and mentor programs, contact
Society of Women Engineers
230 East Ohio Street, Suite 400
Chicago, IL 60611-3265
Tel: 312-596-5223
Email: hq@swe.org
http://www.swe.org

Toxicologists

OVERVIEW

Toxicologists design and conduct studies to determine the potential toxicity of substances to humans, plants, and animals. They provide information on the hazards of these substances to the federal government, private businesses, and the public. Toxicologists may suggest alternatives to using products that contain dangerous amounts of toxins, often by testifying at official hearings. There are an estimated 9,000 toxicologists employed in the United States.

HISTORY

The study of the effects of poisons (toxins) began in the 1500s, when doctors documented changes in body tissues of people who died after a long illness. Although research was hampered by the lack of sophisticated research equipment, physicians and scientists continued to collect information on the causes and effects of various diseases over the next 300 years.

As microscopes and other forms of scientific equipment improved, scientists were able to study in greater detail the impacts of chemicals on the human body and the causes of disease. In the mid-1800s, Rudolf Virchow, a German scientist considered to be the founder of pathology (the study of diseased body tissue), began to unlock the mystery of many diseases by studying tissues at the cellular level. His research of diseased cells helped pathologists pinpoint the paths diseases take in the body.

With society's increasing dependence on chemicals (for example, in agriculture, industry, and medicine) and growing use of prescribed (and illegal) drugs, the study of the impact of these potential toxins on

QUICK FACTS

School Subjects
Biology
Chemistry
Mathematics

Personal Skills
Helping/teaching
Technical/scientific

Work Environment
Primarily indoors
Primarily one location

Minimum Education Level
Bachelor's degree

Salary Range
$35,000 to $70,000 to
$200,000+

Certification or Licensing
Recommended

Outlook
About as fast as the average

DOT
041

GOE
02.03.01

NOC
2121

O*NET-SOC
N/A

public health and environmental quality has become more important. The toxicologist's role in determining the extent of a problem, as well as suggesting possible alternatives or antidotes, plays an important role in society. Toxicologists act as consultants on developing long-term solutions to problems such as air and water pollution, the dumping of toxic waste into landfills, and the recognition of an unusual reaction to a pharmaceutical drug.

THE JOB

As scientists, toxicologists are concerned with the detection and effects of toxins, as well as developing methods to treat intoxication (poisonings). A primary objective of a toxicologist is to protect consumers by reducing the risks of accidental exposure to poisons. Toxicologists investigate the many areas in which our society uses potential toxins and documents their impact. For example, a toxicologist may chemically analyze a fish in a local lake to read for mercury, a harmful toxin to humans if consumed in high enough levels. This reading is reported to government or industry officials, who, in turn, write up a legal policy setting the maximum level of mercury that manufacturing companies can release without contaminating nearby fish and endangering consumers.

On many projects, a toxicologist may be part of a research team, such as at a poison control center or a research laboratory. *Clinical toxicologists* may work to help save emergency drug overdose victims. *Industrial toxicologists* and academic toxicologists work on solving long-term issues, such as studying the toxic effects of cigarettes. They may focus on research and development, working to improve and speed up testing methods without sacrificing safety. Toxicologists use the most modern equipment, such as electron microscopes, atomic absorption spectrometers, and mass spectrometers, and they study new research instrumentation that may help with sophisticated research.

Industrial toxicologists work for private companies, testing new products for potential poisons. For example, before a new cosmetic good can be sold, it must be tested according to strict guidelines. Toxicologists oversee this testing, which is often done on laboratory animals. These toxicologists may apply the test article ingredients topically, orally, or by injection. They test the results through observation, blood analysis, and dissection and detailed pathologic examination. Research results are used for labeling and packaging instructions to ensure that customers use the product safely. Although animal experimentation has created a great deal of controversy with animal-rights supporters, humane procedures are stressed throughout toxicology studies.

Toxicologists carefully document their research procedures so that they can be used in later reports on their findings. They often interact with lawyers and legislators on writing legislation. They may also appear at official hearings designed to discuss and implement new policy decisions.

Because toxic materials are often handled during research and experimentation, a toxicologist must pay careful attention to safety procedures.

REQUIREMENTS

High School

While in high school, you can best prepare for a career as a toxicologist by taking courses in both the physical and biological sciences (chemistry and biology, for example), algebra and geometry, and physics. English and other courses that improve written and verbal communication skills will also be useful, since toxicologists must write and report on complicated study results.

Postsecondary Training

Most toxicologists obtain their undergraduate degrees in a scientific field, such as pharmacology or chemistry. Course work should include mathematics (including mathematical modeling), biology, chemistry, statistics, biochemistry, pathology, anatomy, and research methods.

Career opportunities for graduates with bachelor's degrees are limited; the majority of toxicologists go on to obtain master's or doctorate degrees. Graduate programs vary depending on field of study, but they may include courses such as pathology, environmental toxicology, and molecular biology. Doctorate programs generally last four to five years.

Certification or Licensing

Certification reflects an individual's competence and expertise in toxicology and can enhance career opportunities. The American Board of Toxicology certifies toxicologists after they pass a comprehensive two-day examination and complete the necessary educational requirements. To be eligible, applicants with a bachelor's degree in an appropriate field must first have 10 years of work experience; with a master's degree, seven years; and with a doctorate degree, three years.

Other Requirements

Toxicologists must be hard workers and be dedicated to their field of study. To succeed in their work, they must be careful observers and have an eye for detail. Patience is also necessary, since many research projects can last months to years and show little results. The ability to work both alone and as part of a team is also needed for research.

Because of the nature of their work, toxicologists must also realize the potential dangers of working with hazardous materials. They must also be comfortable working with laboratory animals and be able to dissect them to examine organs and tissues. Though efforts have been made to limit and control live animal experimentation, research still requires their use to identify toxins and, in turn, protect the consumer public.

EXPLORING

If you are interested in pursuing a career as a toxicologist, consider joining a science club in addition to taking biology and chemistry courses to further develop your laboratory skills. Your career counselor might be able to help you arrange a discussion with a practicing toxicologist to explore career options. Part-time jobs in research laboratories or hospitals are an excellent way to explore science firsthand, although opportunities may be limited and require higher levels of education and experience.

EMPLOYERS

According to the Society of Toxicology, approximately 9,000 toxicologists are employed in the United States. A recent job market survey of those with Ph.D.'s shows that 47 percent work for chemical and pharmaceutical companies, 21 percent are employed by large universities or medical schools, and 14 percent work in government. An increasing number (12 percent) work for consulting firms, providing professional recommendations to agencies, industries, and attorneys about issues involving toxic chemicals. Nonprofit research foundations employ only 4 percent of all toxicologists.

STARTING OUT

Those with the necessary education and experience should contact the appropriate research departments in hospitals, colleges and universities, government agencies, or private businesses. Often, school professors and career services advisers provide job leads and recommendations.

Networking with professionals is another useful way to enter the field. Past work with a team of toxicologists during graduate study may open doors to future research opportunities. Membership in a professional society can also offer more networking contacts. In addition, the Society of Toxicology and the American College of Medical Toxicology both offer job placement assistance to members.

ADVANCEMENT

Skilled toxicologists will find many advancement opportunities, although specific promotions depend on the size and type of organization where the toxicologist is employed. Those working for private companies may become heads of research departments. Because of their involvement in developing important company policy, highly skilled and respected toxicologists may become *vice presidents* or *presidents* of companies. Obviously, this type of promotion would entail a change in job responsibilities, involving more administrative tasks than research activities.

Toxicologists working for educational institutions may become professors, heads of a department, or deans. Toxicologists who want to continue to research and teach can advance to positions with higher pay and increased job responsibilities. Toxicologists working at universities usually write grant proposals, teach courses, and train graduate students. University positions often do not pay as well as industrial positions, but they offer more independence in pursuing research interests.

EARNINGS

As trained professionals, toxicologists have good earning potential. Wages vary depending on level of experience, education, and employer. According to the Society of Toxicology, entry-level toxicologists with a Ph.D. earn $35,000 to $60,000. With a Ph.D. and 10 years of experience, toxicologists can earn between $70,000 and $100,000 a year. Toxicologists in executive positions earn more than $100,000, and in the corporate arena they can earn more than $200,000. Those in private industry earn slightly more than those in government or academic positions.

Salaries for toxicologists are, in general, on the rise, but the survey reports that the biggest factor determining earning potential is not location but type of employer. Certification also plays a large role in salary level; toxicologists who are certified earn higher salaries than those who have not earned certification. Comparing gender differences, the salary survey found that women continue to be paid less than their male counterparts.

WORK ENVIRONMENT

Toxicologists usually work in well-equipped laboratories or offices, either as part of a team or alone. Research in libraries or in the field is a major part of the job. Some toxicologists work a standard 40-hour workweek, although many work longer hours. Overtime should be expected if an important research project is on deadline. Research and experimentation can be both physically and mentally tiring, with much of the laboratory work and analysis done while under time restrictions. Some travel may be required to testify at hearings, to collect field samples, or to attend professional conferences.

Toxicologists often work on research that has important health considerations. At a poison control center, for example, toxicologists may try to find information about the poisonous properties of a product while an overdose victim's life is in danger. Because their work involves studying the impact of toxic material, toxicologists must be willing to handle contaminated material and adhere to the strict safety precautions required.

OUTLOOK

Employment opportunities for toxicologists are expected to continue to be good. The growing use of chemicals and pharmaceuticals by society has created demand for trained professionals to determine and limit the health risks associated with potential toxins. In addition, new concerns over bioterrorism and the potential use of chemical weapons will create more demand for toxicologists to help develop new vaccines and other antibiotics. However, according to the Society of Toxicology, the job market for toxicologists, especially in traditional fields, is still expected to be tight.

Job opportunities should be greatest in large urban areas where many large hospitals, chemical manufacturers, and university research facilities are located. Those with the most training and experience will have the best employment prospects.

FOR MORE INFORMATION

For certification information, contact
American Board of Toxicology
PO Box 30054

Raleigh, NC 27622-0054
Tel: 919-841-5022
Email: info@abtox.org
http://www.abtox.org

For information on educational programs and other toxicology resources, contact
American College of Medical Toxicology
1901 North Roselle Road, Suite 920
Schaumburg, IL 60195-3187
Tel: 847-885-0674
Email: info@acmt.net
http://www.acmt.net

For general career information, contact
Society of Toxicology
1821 Michael Faraday Drive, Suite 300
Reston, VA 20190-5342
Tel: 703-438-3115
Email: sothq@toxicology.org
http://www.toxicology.org

Wood Science and Technology Workers

OVERVIEW

Wood scientists and technologists experiment to find the most efficient ways of converting forest resources into useful products for consumers. Toward this end, they explore the physical, biological, and chemical properties of wood and the methods used in growing, processing, and using it. Wood science is conducted for both academic and industrial research and is carried out both in labs and on forest grounds.

HISTORY

Wood is one of the oldest and most versatile raw materials. It has provided shelter, tools, and furniture since prehistoric times. Since the technological revolution, scientists have found ways to treat and process wood in more innovative ways, which has allowed it to be used in many products—everything from plywood to wood plastics—that were unheard of only a few decades ago. From these efforts to find better ways of using wood, the field of wood science technology was developed. Experimentation during World War II marked its modern beginnings, and the field has advanced remarkably since then. Today, more than 5,000 different products use wood as their primary raw material.

Before wood can be used in the making of these products, it must be processed. This can include drying, finishing, seasoning, gluing, machining, or treating for preservation. Wood scientists and technologists study these techniques, in conjunction with the chemical and structural properties of wood, to discover new ways to utilize and enhance wood's strength, endurance, and versatility.

Like metallurgy and plastics manufacturing, wood science is concerned with materials engineering. While wood is one of the earth's few renewable resources, it must be wisely grown, harvested, and used to maximize its benefit. Lumber companies have to plan when and which trees to harvest, and what types of trees to plant now for harvesting in 30 years, so as to get the greatest use of the timberlands. Manufacturers of wood products must use the most efficient methods of converting wood into useful products, so as to achieve the least amount of waste and greatest durability. Wood science helps to fulfill these goals as it works toward more economical and efficient ways to satisfy people's need for wood products.

THE JOB

Some workers in wood science and technology are involved in research. They work for large wood product firms, universities, or the government on various research projects, ranging from the development of new wood plastics to the designing of methods to cut wood without producing sawdust. Tim Murphy, project manager for Aspen Research Corporation, is one such researcher.

Murphy's company is a contract research firm that researches and designs products for other companies. He works in the forest products division, where he and his team of scientists and engineers take on various projects all aimed at making better use of wood products. "Primarily what we work with are engineered wood composites," Murphy says. "In trying to develop a better product for our clients, we focus on a number of specific scientific challenges." Depending on the product under development, Murphy's team might try to enhance the wood's strength or impact resistance by adding fiberglass, adhesives, or polymers to the processed wood.

Another area of work in wood and science technology, which is similar to Murphy's work, is manufacturing. This is the most diverse area of the field, with jobs encompassing product and process development, quality control, production control, engineering, personnel relations, and general management.

Some wood and science technology careers are in the area of technical service. Technical service representatives for wood industry suppliers use their knowledge of wood to enhance the efficiency of their clients' operations. They may work for a chemical company, a machinery manufacturer, or another service-oriented business. State and federal governments also hire workers in this capacity.

Specialists who work in these areas typically fall into one of three categories of workers: *wood scientists, wood technologists* or *wood products engineers,* and *wood products technicians.*

Wood scientists explore the chemical, biological, and physical properties of different woods. They try to find ways to make wood last longer and work better. They also look for faster, more efficient ways to turn wood into lumber, plywood, chemicals, paper, and other products. For example, they develop and improve ways to season or chemically treat wood to increase its resistance to wear, fire, fungi, decay, insects, or marine borers.

All wood must be dried before it can be put to any permanent use in construction or furniture. Wood scientists experiment with methods of drying or curing wood, firing it in kilns at different temperatures and for varying lengths of time, to find ways that will save energy and toughen the wood against warping and other defects.

Because of their thorough knowledge of the properties of different types of wood—pliability, strength, and resistance to wear—wood scientists are able to recommend which woods are most appropriate for certain uses. They can tell what hard and soft woods will make useful lumber and what fast-growing trees can be harvested for plywood and particleboard.

While wood scientists often work in the research area of the industry, wood technologists work primarily for industry. Like scientists, they are also knowledgeable about the scientific properties of wood, but they look at the subject from a business perspective. These specialists work toward finding new ways to make wood products, with a minimum waste of wood, time, and money. Their jobs may combine responsibilities in areas that are usually considered the exclusive domain of either business or science, including materials engineering, research, quality control, production, management, marketing, or sales. "In this field, you really have to want to be involved in both science and business," Murphy says. "Normally, scientists don't have anything to do with business, so this is kind of an interesting blend."

In many ways, wood technologists carry on the work of the wood scientists, by investigating the differing qualities of woods. As employees of paper mills, sawmills, or plywood mills, they may test woods as well as new kilns and new sawmill machines. They may cooperate with *foresters* who grow and harvest wood. If working for a wood products manufacturer, technologists may experiment with new methods of drying, joining, gluing, machining, and finishing lumber. In many cases, they also direct and oversee the activity of other workers, accumulate and analyze data, and write reports.

Wood technologists also work closely with their clients, who may be wood manufacturers or the buyers and distributors of wood products. If a sporting goods manufacturer is looking for light, resilient woods for making skis, for example, the wood technologist machines, treats, and supplies this wood. The technologist may even direct scientific research into new methods of improving the quality of wood for making skis. The wood technologist also knows how to test the wood for the qualities the buyer needs. New tooling machines may need to be designed, new processing techniques might need to be perfected, and workers may need to be hired or specially trained to accomplish the end goal. The wood technologist often coordinates all of these activities for both the company's purposes and the advancement of wood science.

Wood technologists often oversee the work of wood products technicians, who also add to the efficiency and profitability of their companies through their knowledge of wood and its properties. Wood products technicians operate kilns, plywood presses, and other machines used in the processing and treating of wood. They may also work in product testing and quality control, helping technologists and engineers overcome problems and expand the horizons of wood science.

Almost all careers in wood science and technology involve a substantial amount of paperwork. Project documentation, as with any scientific study, is extensive and constant. "The people on my team spend about 50 percent of their time actually in the lab, and the other half of the time on project communications, proposal writing, design layout, and process studies," Murphy says.

REQUIREMENTS

Because of the variety of work done in wood science, there are several academic paths that can be taken to prepare for a career in this field. Almost all of these jobs, however, require education after high school.

High School

Many different specialties are contained within the wood science field. Therefore, a broad understanding of many subjects will prove more useful than extensive study of a single discipline.

Because careers in wood science and technology are heavily scientific in nature, you should take as many high school science classes as possible. Biology, chemistry, and earth sciences are likely to be especially helpful. Mathematics is another important focus area for career preparation. Many jobs in this industry are engineering jobs, which require a solid grasp of advanced math skills. Because both written and oral communication plays such a role in scientific research, English and speech classes are good choices to help you develop these skills.

Postsecondary Training

A bachelor's degree is required for employment as a wood scientist or wood technician. Tim Murphy obtained both a bachelor of science degree in wood science and production management and an associate's degree in natural resources. He received his degrees from the University of Minnesota, one of a number of colleges in the United States that offer degrees in wood science, wood technology, forestry, or forest products (visit http://www.swst.org for a list of programs). Courses of study in these programs may include wood physics, wood chemistry, wood-fluid relationships, wood machinery, and production management. Degree programs in chemistry, biology, physics, mechanical engineering, materials science, or civil engineering can also be very useful if combined with courses in wood science.

A master's degree or doctorate is usually required for more advanced work as a researcher. Advanced studies include such topics as pulp and paper science, business administration, production management, and forestry-wood sciences. Murphy says that the majority of the researchers in his department have master's degrees. "Advanced education is common in the research end of the business," he says.

Apprenticeships used to be the most common method of training for wood products technicians, but today most earn a certificate or associate's degree from a two-year college. Their course work in wood science includes the identification, composition, and uses of wood. It also covers wood design, manufacturing, seasoning and machining, and methods and materials for making wood products. Some business courses may also be included. Some students may wish to earn a two-year degree first and then transfer to another school to earn a bachelor's degree. "It's possible to get a job as a lab technician with an associate's degree," Murphy says, "but the career path for those people is really pretty limited."

Other Requirements

The main personal requirement for success in this field is the ability to communicate well. "You really have to be able to communicate quickly and effectively, both with your mouth and on paper," Tim Murphy says. "You also need to have an enjoyment of the sciences and the desire to be in business."

The ability to understand and use scientific theory is important in this career, as are curiosity and persistence in your work habits. Finally, an interest in wood and conservation issues is a plus. Workers in this industry should be environmentally aware, as their industry is contingent on the preservation and proper use of wood as a renewable resource.

EXPLORING

High school guidance counselors should be able to provide you with literature and information on careers in this field. If you live near a college that offers a wood science and technology degree, or near a logging industry or manufacturer of wood products, you may be able to talk with students, professors, or employees who can explain the field more fully. It may even be possible to find a part-time or summer job in the wood industry. Finally, any experience in working with wood and wood products will provide you with valuable insight and education. If there are woodworking classes offered in your high school or community, you might consider taking them. By working with wood, you can begin to understand the differences in wood types and how they respond to various kinds of woodworking procedures.

EMPLOYERS

Most wood scientists and technologists are employed in private industry. Firms dealing with forest products, such as mills, manufacturers of wood products, suppliers to the wood products industry, forest products associations, and paper and pulp companies all hire these kinds of workers. Independent contract research firms, like Tim Murphy's company, may also be sources of employment. Universities and federal and state agencies, such as agricultural extension services, hire wood science and technology experts to work on various research projects.

Geographically, careers in wood science and technology tend to be situated near large wood-producing forests and mills. Most wood science technologists work along the Eastern Seaboard, in the North Central States, in the Pacific Northwest, and in the southern states from Virginia to eastern Texas.

STARTING OUT

Tim Murphy feels that wood science and technology jobs are not hard for qualified applicants to come by. "I was at the University

The Many Uses of Wood

Wood provides us with countless resources that we use in our every-day lives. In fact, more than 5,000 different products use wood as their primary raw material. Here are just a few of the diverse products created from wood and paper:

Products from Solid Wood
- Baseball bats
- Guitars
- Birdhouses
- Charcoal
- Furniture
- Lumber and plywood used in home construction

Paper Products
- Coffee filters
- Books
- Newspapers
- Building insulation
- Computer paper
- Milk cartons

Products from Tree Extracts
- Cereals
- Vegetarian foods
- Cleaning products

- Deodorants
- Colognes
- Medicine to treat high blood pressure, Parkinson's Disease, and other illnesses

Bark
- Cancer-fighting drugs
- Cosmetics
- Shoe polish
- Cinnamon
- Cork
- Garden mulch

Cellulose
- Toothpaste
- Floor tiles
- Luggage
- Antacids
- Rayon clothing
- Carpeting

Source: National Hardwood Lumber Association

of Minnesota, and a company contacted me and hired me right out of the university," he says. "The companies really recruited us heavily."

This is not uncommon. Many forestry firms recruit new employees during visits to campus, and new graduates of wood science and technology programs often learn about employment opportunities through their colleges' career services offices. Other sources of information are professional groups, which may maintain job referral or resume services, and trade magazines, which often carry want ads for job openings. Information on jobs with the federal government can be obtained from the Office of Personnel Management (http://www.usajobs.opm.gov).

ADVANCEMENT

Moving ahead in the wood science field depends on ingenuity, skills, and the ability to handle important projects. There is no typical career path, and advancement can come in the form of promotions, pay raises, or more important assignments. People with management skills may rise to become sales managers, division chiefs, or directors, although the size of the company often dictates the opportunities for advancement. Larger companies obviously offer more places within the organization, so advancement may be quicker than in a smaller company.

An advanced degree, such as a master's or a Ph.D., can be the ticket to advancement for those working in research; workers in this field may be granted permission to conduct independent research or be promoted to heads of research operations. Wood science and technology employees in the business area of the industry may find that additional schooling makes them better candidates for higher administrative positions. Wood products technicians may find that earning a bachelor's degree can help them move up to the position of wood technologist.

EARNINGS

Salary levels in the wood sciences depend on the individual's employer, experience, level of education, and work performed. Average starting salaries for graduates with bachelor's degrees in wood science are approximately $50,000 to $55,000. Those with M.B.A.'s can earn $74,000 or more, and very experienced professionals in the wood science field can make well over $100,000 a year.

Workers in the private sector earn slightly higher starting salaries. Wages for beginning wood products technicians are somewhat less, with average salaries in the range of $34,000 to $37,000.

Usually wood scientists, wood technologists, and wood products technicians receive fringe benefits, including health insurance, pension plans, and paid vacations.

WORK ENVIRONMENT

Depending on the type of work they perform, wood science specialists operate in a variety of settings, from the office to the open forest. Wood scientists and researchers work in laboratories and, if they are on university faculty, in classrooms. Their experimental work may take them to tree farms and forests. Wood technologists and technicians may work in offices, manufacturing plants, sawmills, or research facilities. Those technologists who are involved in sales often need to travel.

Work may be solitary or as part of a team, depending on the position and the project. And workers in the lab may use a wide variety of equipment—anything from a table saw to a word processing program to a chemical analytical device, according to Tim Murphy.

These types of employees work a normal 40-hour week, but extra hours may be required in certain situations. Technologists who supervise technicians and other production workers may have to work second and third shifts. Administrators may also have to put in extra hours. Workers paid by the hour often get overtime pay, but salaried employees do not get extra monetary compensation for their extra hours.

Wood science and technology specialists have a difficult but rewarding job: applying scientific principles such as chemistry, physics, and mathematics to a commonplace raw material and finding new ways for society to use wood in more productive, efficient ways. Many who work in this field enjoy the challenge it presents and feel fulfilled by helping to better understand and more efficiently utilize one of the earth's most necessary resources.

OUTLOOK

Wood technology is a relatively new science, with breakthroughs in products and technology occurring frequently. It is also a field in which the supply of qualified wood scientists and technologists is short of the demand. Therefore, the employment outlook for these workers in this field is expected to be very good. There is a national average of three job offers for every new wood science graduate.

The demand for wood products is increasing rapidly. At the same time, the costs of growing and harvesting timber and processing wood products are rising rapidly. Wood manufacturers need the skills of wood science specialists to keep their operations profitable and efficient and to help them compete with plastics manufacturers and the makers of other wood substitutes. "There's a lot of activity in this field right now because of the shortage of wood products," Tim Murphy says. "Companies are spending more money on product development in this area."

Conservation programs will affect the industry both positively and negatively. Pressure to reduce lumber harvests will continue to increase, particularly in threatened areas, such as the rainforest. Those pressures, however, will force increased study of ways to better utilize wood currently being harvested. "The main thrust of the industry right now is to use everything the tree has to offer," Murphy says. "What we're trying to do is to optimize utilization of wood."

Although the employment outlook for wood science and technology workers is expected to be strong, it is heavily tied to the overall economy. Because the bulk of all forest products is used in the construction industry, a downturn in new construction means a downturn in all forest-related careers. "Our industry is tightly linked to the housing index," Murphy says. "When those start to go down, you get nervous about your job. It can be a roller coaster ride with the economy."

FOR MORE INFORMATION

For technical periodicals, newsletters, and directories covering a broad range of topics related to wood and wood fiber properties, products, and markets, contact
Forest Products Society
2801 Marshall Court
Madison, WI 53705-2295
Tel: 608-231-1361
Email: info@forestprod.org
http://www.forestprod.org

For information on education programs and publications, contact
National Hardwood Lumber Association
6830 Raleigh-LaGrange Road
Memphis, TN 38184-0518
Tel: 901-377-1818
Email: info@nhla.com
http://www.natlhardwood.org

For a career packet and a listing of job opportunities and employers in the area of wood science and technology, contact
Society of American Foresters
5400 Grosvenor Lane
Bethesda, MD 20814-2198
Tel: 301-897-8720
Email: safweb@safnet.org
http://www.safnet.org

For a brochure or video on careers, or a listing of schools offering degrees in wood science and technology, contact
Society of Wood Science and Technology
One Gifford Pinchot Drive

Madison, WI 53726-2398
Tel: 608-231-9347
http://www.swst.org

*For information on marketing and manufacturing careers in wood
products in Canada, and distance learning, contact*
Canadian Wood Council
99 Bank Street, Suite 400
Ottawa, ON K1P 6B9 Canada
Tel: 800-463-5091
Email: info@cwc.ca
http://www.cwc.ca

───────── INTERVIEW ─────────

*Dr. Thomas McLain, professor and head of the Department of
Wood Science and Engineering at Oregon State University in Cor-
vallis, Oregon, discussed his career and wood science technology
with the editors of* Careers in Focus: Chemistry.

Q. Why did you decide to pursue a career in wood science?

A. Like many wood science and technology majors I started off
being interested in forestry. However, I soon discovered that I
didn't really like the cold and wet part of working outdoors, and
that I really liked science, especially chemistry. I took several
wood science classes that exposed me to the incredible complexity of wood, and I became very interested in the science of
natural materials and how they could be used to make useful
things. That led to a bachelor of science in wood science and
technology. Summer jobs and other life experiences led me to
graduate school where I learned how the chemistry, mechanical
properties, and anatomy of wood dictate the various ways that
humans use the material. Eventually, I focused my efforts on
the mechanical and engineering properties of wood and wood-
based materials and graduated with a Ph.D. from a program that
blended wood science with civil engineering. After a few years
working as an engineer in the private sector I became a university professor where for the past 30 years I have been a teacher,
researcher, and administrator.

Q. Please tell us about your program.

A. Oregon State University (OSU) is the home to one of the largest comprehensive wood science and technology programs in

North America. We offer a bachelor of science in wood science and technology and master's of science and Ph.D. degrees in wood science. Our program is comprehensive, and we prepare students for challenging and diverse careers in business, science, engineering, or technology related to the manufacture and use of solid wood and wood-based composite materials. Visit http://woodscience.oregonstate.edu to learn more about the program.

Q. What is one thing that young people may not know about a career in wood science and technology?

A. The career opportunities are incredibly diverse, highly challenging, well paid, and far ranging. Graduates work in rural locations, cities, and, increasingly, in foreign countries. Their workplace may be manufacturing plants, business offices, research labs, government offices, or job sites. Most work tends to be hands on.

Q. For what type of jobs does your program prepare students?

A. Typical entry-level and early career jobs with a bachelor of science in wood science and technology are in:

1) Manufacturing—product and process development, quality control, production, and management. Entry level-positions are typically in production and management training. Examples might include production supervisor in a sawmill or composite panel plant.

2) Marketing is essential to business and deals with many activities connected with the flow and exchange of ideas, goods, and services from initial concept to consumer use. Entry-level positions are often in sales, advertising, and management training. There is a very high demand for marketing people who have a strong science background.

3) Technical service providers work for manufacturers, suppliers, or industry associations and use their knowledge of wood and the industry to enhance the efficiency or profitability of clients, or to provide technical advice and solve industry or consumer problems. University extension programs are another source of employment.

4) Research and development workers use imagination, inquisitiveness, and insight to solve problems or discover new ideas or products. Research areas are many, especially with material development and behavior, or process improvement. These careers may require graduate degrees.

Some entry-level job titles of recent graduates include:

plant engineer	research technologist
research general engineer	wood products
resin chemist	pathologist
design engineer	editor, trade journal
wood products	trade association
technologist	representative
project engineer	product development
sales manager	specialist
wood chemist	management trainee
products manager	account representative
marketing manager	wood technologist
technical support writer	software analyst
quality control supervisor	quality control technician
technical director	extension agent
technical service manager	research scientist
international lumber trader	total quality trainee

Q. What is the employment outlook for wood science and technology graduates?

A. One hundred percent of OSU wood science and technology (WS&T) majors who look for jobs after graduating easily find them. This is true for WS&T majors in other programs in North America as well. It is not unusual for a graduate to receive three to five job offers, especially if they are not geographically constrained. Why is that? Wood is the most abundant, useful, and greenest natural material in the world, and we use more of it than we do of plastics, steel, and cement combined each year to make over 5,000 different products! Concerns about sustainability and global warming mean that we will use even more in the future, especially in composite materials.

Q. What are the most promising career areas?

A. There are many jobs in all sectors of the wood products industry. The greatest future demand in North America, however, will be in composite materials manufacturing, marketing, and sales of all products, especially international, technical services at all levels and research and development.

Index

Entries and page numbers in **bold** indicate major treatment of a topic.

Q
quality control engineers and
technicians 167–176
quality control technicians 111

R
Rader's CHEM4KIDS! 45
research chief engineer 130–131
research engineers 26–27
research specialists 160
reservoir engineering technicians
142
reservoir engineers 130
rotary drillers 139–140
Rush, Benjamin 55

S
safety engineer 104
Schleiden, Matthias 14
Schmiedeberg, Oswald 150
Schwann, Theodor 14
Society of American Foresters 193
Society of Cosmetic Chemists 53
Society of Forensic Toxicologists
92
Society of Manufacturing Engineers
30, 33–34
Society of Petroleum Engineers
134, 137, 148
Society of Plastic Engineers (SPE)
162, 163, 166
Society of the Plastics Industry
(SPI) 161, 162, 166
Society of Toxicology 180, 181,
182, 183
Society of Women Engineers (SWE)
30, 34, 137, 166, 176
Society of Wood Science and
Technology 193–194
soil pollution technicians 67,
69–70
Swammerdam, Jan 118

T
technical sales engineers 28
tissue technicians 120
tool pushers 139–140
toxicologists 177–183
treaters 141

U
U.S. Department of Agriculture
12, 42, 50, 69, 80, 82
U.S. Department of Energy 50, 69
U.S. Department of Health and
Human Services 42, 50
U.S. Department of Interior 69
United Steel, Paper and Forestry,
Rubber, Manufacturing, Energy,
Allied-Industrial and Service
Workers International Union 98
United Steelworkers of America 98
University of Illinois at Urbana-
Champaign 82–84
University of Texas at Austin 148

V
veterinary pharmacologists 151
vice presidents (of companies) 181
Virchow, Rudolf 177

W
Water Environment Federation 73
water pollution technicians 66, 69
Watson, James 14
well loggers 141
well-servicing technicians 141
wood products engineers 186
wood products technicians 186
wood science and technology
workers 184–196
wood scientists 186
wood technologists 186
Worcester Polytechnic Institute
133, 137